ENIGMATIC EVENTS

UNSOLVED HISTORY

ENIGMATIC
EVENTS

GARY L. BLACKWOOD

 **Marshall Cavendish**
Benchmark
New York

Benchmark Books
Marshall Cavendish
99 White Plains Road
Tarrytown, New York 10591-9001
www.marshallcavendish.us

All Internet sites were available and accurate when this book was sent to press.

Book design by Michael Nelson

Library of Congress Cataloging-in-Publication Data
Blackwood, Gary L.
Enigmatic events / by Gary L. Blackwood.
p. cm.—(Unsolved history)
Summary: Explores several events that have baffled scientists and historians for years,
such as the demise of dinosaurs, the "lost colony" of Roanoke, the sinking of the Maine,
and the Hindenburg disaster.—Provided by publisher.
Includes bibliographical references (p.) and index.
ISBN 0-7614-1889-X
1. History—Miscellanea—Juvenile literature. 2. Disasters—Juvenile literature.
3. Curiosities and wonders—Juvenile literature. I. Title.
D24.B58 2005
904—dc22
2004023755

Illustrations provided by Rose Corbett Gordon, Art Editor, Mystic CT, from the following sources:
Front cover: Royalty-Free/Corbis Back cover: Bettmann/Corbis Pages i, 6,7: DK Images; page iii: Kactus
Foto/SuperStock; pages iii, vi: Private Collection/Bridgeman Art Library; page viii: Julian Baum/Photo
Researchers, Inc.; page 2: John B. Sibbick; pages 4, 5: D. van Ravenswaay/ Photo Researchers, Inc.; page 8:
Claus Lunau/FOCI/Bonnier Pub./Photo Researchers, Inc.; pages 10, 24, 25: The Art Archive; page 12:
Stapleton Collection/Corbis; page 13: Kunstbibliothek, Staatliche Museen zu Berlin Bildarchiv Preussischer
Kulturbesitz/Art Resource, NY; pages 14, 15, 38, 39, 40, 42, 52, 59: The Granger Collection, New York; page
17: The Mariners' Museum/Corbis; page 20: New-York Historical Society/ Bridgeman Art Library; page 23, 27:
Massachusetts Historical Society, Boston/ Bridgeman Art Library; page 26: Peabody Essex Museum/Bridgeman
Art Library; pages 28, 30, 32, 33, 34: Photograph Courtesy of the Peabody Essex Museum; page 31: Atlantic
Mutual Insurance Company; pages 36, 41, 50, 54, 57 bottom: Bettmann/Corbis; page 44: Erich Schrempp/
Photo Researchers, Inc.; page 47: Sovfoto/Eastfoto; page 49: Astrofoto/van Ravenswaay/Koch / Peter Arnold,
Inc.; pages 55, 57 top, 60: Navy Lakehurst Historical Society; page 57 middle: Corbis.

Printed in Malaysia
135642

Front cover: *Head Behind a Brick Wall* by Jane Marinsky
Back cover: Nikola Tesla in his laboratory
Half title page: One small victim of the great extinction
Title page: *Veil of Sadness,* by Wayne Anderson, 1980
Introduction, page vi: Illustration by Howard Pyle from "The Salem Wolf," Harper's Magazine, 1909

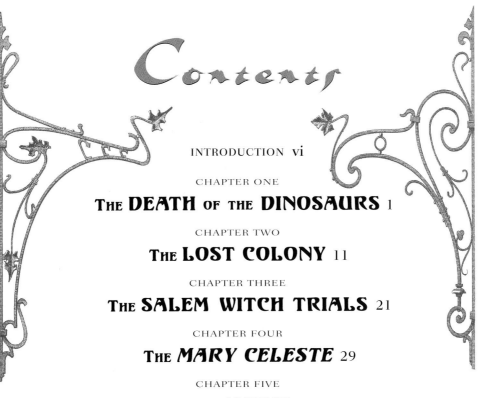

Contents

INTRODUCTION

This is a book about catastrophes. The catastrophes recounted here, however, aren't necessarily history's most devastating ones. In fact, with the exception of the great Cretaceous extinction—which scientist Robert Bakker calls "the grandest evolutionary disaster of all time"—they're all fairly minor, at least in terms of lives lost.

Not many of these calamities had a major impact on the course of history, either. Like the people and events that are covered in the other volumes in this series, the cases you'll encounter here were chosen not because of their historical importance but because they've baffled so many scientists and historians for so many years.

The aura of mystery that surrounds them isn't due to any shortage of information. Each of the events is thoroughly documented (again, with the exception of the Cretaceous extinction, which took place long before humans were around to take notes), and every detail about them has been scrutinized and analyzed by dozens of scholars. Yet, for the most part, we don't seem to be any closer to understanding how or why they happened—or, in some cases, exactly *what* happened.

Several of the events have been written about so much that you may already be familiar with them to some extent—the Cretaceous extinction, for example, which wiped out the dinosaurs; or the notorious Salem witch trials; or the lost colony of Roanoke. Although some of the other cases are not as well known, they're every bit as fascinating and mysterious. There's the riddle of the *Mary Celeste*, the nineteenth-century sailing ship whose crew unaccountably vanished; the explosion of the battleship *Maine*, which ignited the Spanish-American War; the destruction of the airship *Hindenburg*, which some called an accident and others called sabotage; and the 1908 catastrophe known as the Tunguska event, whose effects were felt halfway around the world but whose cause is still unknown.

Every so often, the media announces that one of these puzzles has been solved to everyone's satisfaction. But, as anthropologist Lee Miller notes, "One great flaw in the writing of history is that we often tend to accept easy explanations of events." Eventually some scientist or historian who is not so easily satisfied comes along and challenges the consensus, setting the controversy in motion all over again—and ensuring that, in the words of another writer, "the miraculous, the mysterious, and the enigmatic are alive and well, and always have been."

CHAPTER
ONE

The DEATH OF THE DINOSAURS

WE TEND TO THINK OF AN EVENT AS A CATASTROPHE only if it affects us humans. But the worst disasters ever to befall the earth happened millions of years before anything remotely resembling *Homo sapiens* came along.

Our planet has suffered at least five great mass extinctions, or die-offs, plus about twenty smaller ones. Science uses the "Big Five" as boundary markers to divide geologic periods from one another. The earliest mass extinction took place about 440 million years ago, at the end of the Ordovician period; it involved mostly simple sea creatures. A second die-off 365 million years ago brought the Devonian period to a close. At the end of the Permian period, 250 million years ago, perhaps 90 percent of the plants and animals on Earth also met their end. A mere 45 million years later, a fourth extinction killed off, among other things, some of the early dinosaurs.

Opposite: Many scientists think that Earth's fifth great mass extinction, which wiped out the dinosaurs, was caused by a comet or meteorite. But some scientists believe that when the deadly extraterrestrial body struck, the dinosaurs were already on their way out.

1

But the "terrible lizards" made a big comeback. According to Dr. Robert Bakker, "If we measured success by longevity, then dinosaurs must rank as the number one success story in the history of land life." They were undisputed rulers of the earth for at least 130 million years. Mammals, by contrast, have been top dog for less than 70 million. As for humans . . . well, we've been on Earth for a paltry 100,000.

Most dinosaur species didn't hang around for the whole 130 million years, of course. They kept evolving and adapting. By the end of the Cretaceous period, about 65 million years ago, there were perhaps twenty species, possibly more, in the western United States alone, including the famous triceratops and tyrannosaurus. What is now the

ENIGMATIC EVENTS

Great Plains was then covered by a shallow, warm inland sea, creating a semitropical climate in which the huge creatures flourished.

Then something happened that radically changed conditions on the earth and brought on what scientists call the "Time of Great Dying." Dinosaurs weren't the only victims, of course. But because they were so big and so well established, it's especially hard to imagine how they could be wiped out so suddenly and completely. In the words of paleontologist John R. Horner, they "seem to have disappeared in the geological equivalent of an instant."

How long it actually took them to die out is a matter of much dispute among scientists. At one end of the spectrum are the so-called catastrophists, who believe it could have happened in ten years or less. At the other end are the gradualists, who suspect it was more in the neighborhood of two million years.

One of the earliest catastrophists was the eighteenth-century French scientist Pierre-Louis de Maupertuis, who suggested that, if a large comet struck the earth, it might well destroy entire species. Half a century later another Frenchman, Baron Georges Cuvier, became an outspoken champion of this theory.

Most of the scientific community, however, sided with English geologist Charles Lyell, who preached that all changes in nature happen in small increments, over long periods of time. The gradualists managed to keep the upper hand for the next century or so.

Judging from the amount of iridium it left, scientists estimate that the Chicxulub meteorite or comet was at least six miles in diameter.

Then, in the mid-1970s, Luis Alvarez, a Nobel Prize-winning physicist, began analyzing samples of rust-colored clay that's found worldwide, sandwiched between limestone from the Cretaceous period and stone formed during the period that followed, the Tertiary—"like jam in a sponge cake," as one writer puts it. Alvarez discovered that the clay contained startlingly high amounts of iridium, a dense element that's rare in the earth's crust but abundant in extraterrestrial bodies—meteors, comets, and asteroids.

He concluded that near the end of the Cretaceous period, a comet or meteorite roughly six miles in diameter struck the earth, throwing up an immense cloud of dust that eventually settled, creating the layer of clay that marked the K-T (Cretaceous-Tertiary) boundary. There was one flaw in the theory, though: an object that size would have left an immense crater, and no one had discovered a crater that was the right size and age.

However, oil companies drilling off the coast of Mexico had long been aware of a curious circular formation on the ocean floor, buried beneath a thick layer of sediment. By the mid-1990s, scientists had identified it as an astrobleme—an eroded impact crater—and dubbed it the Chicxulub (pronounced *chick-shoe-lube*) crater.

ENIGMATIC EVENTS

According to geologist Charles Frankel, "the Chicxulub crater is universally recognized as the source of the K-T boundary clay—and as the likely cause of the great mass extinction." Not quite. There are still plenty of gradualists around and, although they're willing to concede that a comet or meteorite did hit the earth 65 million years ago, they don't believe that it caused the dinosaurs' demise.

The impact carved out a crater 100 miles wide. It probably also created an enormous tsunami, triggered earthquakes and volcanic eruptions, and threw trillions of tons of dust into the atmosphere.

Even among scientists who *do* believe it, there's a great deal of disagreement over just how the impact affected the dinosaurs. Some say that the cloud of dust blocked the sun for so long that it brought on an "impact winter," a global cooling trend. As plant life, deprived of sunlight—and perhaps pelted by acid rain—died off, so did the herbivorous dinosaurs that fed on it and so, in turn, did the carnivorous dinosaurs that fed on them.

Another scenario assumes just the opposite—that the shroud of dust created a greenhouse effect, raising the temperature of the earth. As the oceans warmed, the plankton died off, as did the creatures that fed on it, and so on up the food chain.

The gradualists don't buy either of these theories. Many of them believe that the dinosaurs were already a dying breed and that the Chicxulub event, at most, simply hastened their end. They place the blame on other factors, most notably what's called the Bearpaw regression. At the end of the Cretaceous, parts of the ocean floor were sinking; at the same time, the Rocky Mountains were rising. As a result, the shallow sea that covered most of North America slowly drained away, leaving behind a virtual desert that couldn't support such large creatures.

It's possible, of course, that it was neither an extraterrestrial object nor the receding seas that did the dinosaurs in. As Robert Bakker points out, "The mass murder that marked the end of the Cretaceous Period seems to attract all manner of solutions." Some are more credible than others. Here are a few of the most interesting:

"Extinction," writes author John Noble Wilford, "is the fate of all species."

• Gases from volcanic eruptions destroyed the ozone

ENIGMATIC EVENTS

layer, giving the dinosaurs unhealthy doses of ultraviolet rays.

• A supernova—an exploding star—bombarded them with cosmic radiation.

• Because they had poor tastebuds, they ate toxic plants that poisoned them.

• Insects or parasites spread disease among them.

• Their eggs were eaten by the crafty mammals that had begun to appear.

• The shells of their eggs grew too thin as a result of stress from overpopulation.

• Alien spacecraft brought safaris here from other planets to hunt them.

• They drowned in the biblical flood because there was no room for them on the ark.

• They were so overcome with boredom that they committed mass suicide.

One extinction theory holds that early mammals, like these primitive rodents, ate the dinosaurs' eggs.

The Shiva Hypothesis

Scientists who favor the catastrophe theory have observed that Earth's mass extinctions seem to follow a sort of timetable: the intervals between them are always around 26 to 32 million years. This has led astronomers to formulate what is familiarly called the "Shiva hypothesis," named after the Hindu god of destruction and renewal.

According to the Shiva hypothesis, every 30 million years or so something disturbs the trillions of comets that circle the sun at the outer limits of the solar system, in a formation known as the Oort cloud. A large number of the icy bodies, dislodged from their orbits, hurtle toward the sun. Along the way, a few strike the planets.

There are all sorts of conjectures about what it is that shakes the comets loose. Probably the most popular theory is that our sun has a dim companion star whose path periodically takes it through the Oort cloud. Although this celestial body has yet to be found, it's been given the Star Trekish name of Nemesis. Another possibility is Planet X, a theoretical tenth planet that follows an erratic orbit somewhere out beyond Pluto.

It may be wrong, though, to pin the blame on an undiscovered planet or star. The real culprit may be something less substantial. As our solar system circles the Milky Way, it drifts up and down, a movement known as galactic oscillation. In doing so, it periodically passes through clumps of dust and gas called interstellar clouds. Some astronomers feel these clouds may be dense enough to deflect comets from their orbits. There's no real proof that they do, but it is intriguing to note that we encounter the heaviest concentration of interstellar clouds once every 33 million years.

Opposite: The Oort cloud lies some 50,000 times farther from the sun than the earth does. The cloud may be made up of materials left over from the formation of the solar system.

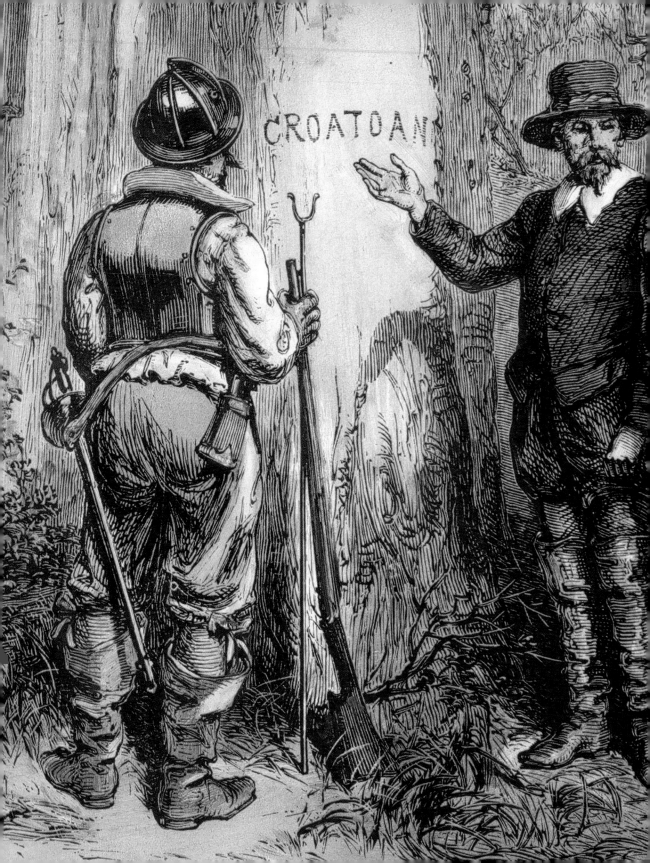

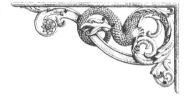

The LOST COLONY

THERE ARE A NUMBER OF OTHER UNANSWERED
questions about the dinosaurs. For example, no one is quite
certain whether they were warm-blooded, like mammals
and birds, or cold-blooded, like reptiles and amphibians, or
something in between.

But such matters are mainly the province of paleontol-
ogists. Historians are more concerned with the affairs of
humans. And when it comes to being mysterious, people
have it all over the dinosaurs.

Human beings usually have rather complex reasons for
their actions, reasons that may be hard for us, looking back
from a distance of decades or centuries, to fathom. And,
unlike most other forms of life, humans can be deliberately
deceptive, even deliberately destructive.

Naturally, the more people involved in a historical

Opposite: The riddle
of the lost colony
of Roanoke has
fascinated countless
writers and illustrators,
including the 19th-
century artist who
made this engraving.

11

Though Elizabeth loved flirting with handsome courtiers and encouraged a long succession of suitors, she preferred to rule England alone.

event, the greater the possibility that one or more of them is up to no good. The story of the lost colony of Roanoke features a huge cast of characters that includes such sixteenth-century English celebrities as Sir Walter Raleigh, Sir Francis Drake, John Smith, and Queen Elizabeth I—plus some who were not so well known but just as influential.

The term *lost* implies that the Roanoke settlers unaccountably vanished. But some historians believe that their attempt to start a colony in America was doomed from the outset, that those lesser-known but influential people were doing their best to make sure it didn't succeed.

In 1584, Queen Elizabeth granted her favorite courtier, Sir Walter Raleigh, an exclusive patent to colonize the newly claimed territory of Virginia, which theoretically included all of North America not already occupied by Spain.

Raleigh was perhaps less interested in actually settling

ENIGMATIC EVENTS

the New World than he was in establishing a base from which he could raid Spanish ships laden with treasure from Mexico. He sent a small expedition to scout the area south of Chesapeake Bay. The native people there were, according to the expedition's leader, "most gentle, loving and faithful, void of all guile and treason," and the offshore islands were "most beautiful and pleasant to behold . . . full of currants, of flax and many other notable commodities."

In the summer of 1585, Raleigh financed a second expedition, led by his cousin Sir Richard Grenville. The party set out for Virginia with seven ships and a hundred colonists. Things didn't go so smoothly this time. The group's sailing master, a former pirate named Simon Fernandes, ran one of the ships aground, ruining the supplies it carried. Plants and animals weren't as abundant as the previous expedition had

This 1590 engraving shows English ships—including several wrecked ones—off the coast of Virginia. Notice the sea monster.

Sir Richard Grenville was far more eager to attack Spanish treasure ships than he was to establish a colony.

reported. Relations with the native people weren't so amiable, either. When Grenville suspected the Indians of stealing a silver cup, he took his revenge by burning their village.

After Grenville returned to England for supplies, matters grew even worse for the colonists he left behind. A drought withered the crops. The Indians began dying off, probably from some disease carried by the Europeans. Their *werowance,* or chief, Wingina, made plans to attack the intruders, but the English struck first and killed him.

In June 1586, Sir Francis Drake sailed into the area, fresh from a raid on Spanish territory. Finding Grenville's men short on food and surrounded by hostile Indians, he offered them a ride home. When Grenville arrived with supplies, the settlement was deserted. To keep England's tenuous hold on the area, he left fifteen men on Roanoke Island, off the coast of what is now North Carolina.

The following summer, Raleigh sent a company of 117 colonists with instructions to settle the area around Chesapeake Bay. Their leader was John White, an artist and mapmaker who had been with Grenville's expedition. Among them were seventeen women—including White's daughter, Eleanor Dare—and nine children.

The sailing master was Simon Fernandes, the former pirate who had run Grenville's ship aground. Off the Portuguese coast, one of the expedition's three ships had some sort of trouble. According to White, Fernandes "lewdly forsook [wickedly abandoned]" the unfortunate vessel, "leaving her distressed." White began to suspect that Fernandes was purposely sabotaging the expediton.

It seemed he was right. Instead of sailing directly to their destination, Fernandes went by way of the West Indies. The colonists, who were running low on food, asked Fernandes to take on fresh supplies, but he refused. By the time they finally headed for Chesapeake Bay, the summer was far gone.

Though Raleigh's attempts to settle the New World nearly bankrupted him, he never visited the colony himself.

They made a stop at Roanoke Island to pick up the men Grenville had left. But "we found none of them, nor any signe, that they had bene there, saving onely we found the bones of one of those fifteene, which the Savages had slaine." Then one of White's party, who had wandered off, was found dead, his body bristling with arrows.

The colonists were eager to go on to Chesapeake Bay, but Fernandes announced that it was too late in the year; they would have to winter on Roanoke. It was too late for them to plant crops, too. Desperate, the company asked White to

return to England and fetch more provisions. White was reluctant, especially since his daughter had just given birth to a child, appropriately named Virginia. But when the colonists "earnestly entreated," he agreed. He instructed them that if for some reason they left Roanoke, they were to post a sign indicating where they had gone, and "if they should happen to be distressed . . . they should carve over the letters or name, a Crosse."

White reached England in November and met with Raleigh, who promised that "he would prepare a good supply . . . of all things needful which he intended, God willing, should be with [the colonists] the summer following." But Queen Elizabeth, fearing an attack by the Spanish fleet, called the Armada, ordered all English ships to stay close to home, in case they were needed for defense. Although Raleigh noted that "there is little regard taken of the general restraint," White couldn't find a ship to take him to Virginia until March 1590.

Unfortunately its captain was a privateer whose priority was not rescuing settlers but chasing Spanish treasure ships. White didn't reach Roanoke until the middle of August—almost exactly three years after leaving his company in such dire straits. There was no sign of life on the island. "We found the houses taken downe, and . . . things, throwen here and there, almost overgrowen with grasse and weeds."

On a post nearby "in fayre Capitall letters was graven CROATOAN without any crosse or signe of distresse."

White took this to mean that the colonists had relocated to Croatoan Island, about fifty miles to the south. The English had somehow managed to remain on friendly terms with the Indians there.

White convinced the sailors to take him to Croatoan. But a fierce storm drove the ship so far off course that the captain changed his mind. To White's dismay, they headed home, "thus committing the relief of my discomfortable company the planters in Virginia, to the merciful help of the Almighty."

During his first trip to Virginia, John White spent much of his time taking notes and painting pictures like this one of a man identified as "A Chief Lord of Roanoke."

Raleigh dispatched no fewer than five separate expeditions in an attempt to learn the fate of the colony. But "the parties by him set forth performed nothing." Still, it was generally assumed that the Virginia settlers were alive. In a play from the period, *Eastward Hoe,* one of the characters says, "A whole country of English is there, man, bred of those that were left there in '87; they have married with the Indians."

When the Jamestown colonists arrived in the New World in 1607, the local Indians told them that the Roanoke company—or at least part of it—had come north to Chesapeake Bay. There they were attacked by hostile tribes under the command of a chief named

Wahunsonacock (called Powhatan by the Europeans, and best known as the father of Pocahontas), and "miserably slaughtered."

If so, some may have survived the massacre, for the Jamestowners also heard stories of men living inland who wore European-style clothing, lived in "howses built with stone walls, and one story above another," and had "haire of a perfect yellow and a reasonable white skinne." Several parties were sent to search for these "White Indians," without success. "And thus we left seeking our colony," wrote one of the settlers, "that was never any of them found, nor seen to this day."

In 1701 surveyor John Lawson visited Croatoan Island. The Indians there claimed that "several of their ancestors were white people . . . the truth of which is confirmed by grey eyes being found frequently amongst these Indians." Later, settlers along the Lumber River in North Carolina also encountered gray-eyed Indians; some had surnames that matched those of the lost colonists.

Of course, the "White Indians" in these accounts were not necessarily Roanoke colonists or their descendants. Plenty of other Europeans had been stranded on the shores of the New World, including shipwrecked sailors and Spanish soldiers, not to mention the fourteen men left by Grenville whose bodies were never found.

Some scholars suggest that the Roanoke settlers built a ship and tried to sail home but were lost at sea. Others think the settlement could have been discovered by

Spanish soldiers, who captured or killed the English.

If the colonists were, in fact, massacred by Indians, it may not have been the Indians of Chesapeake Bay who were responsible, but those in the Roanoke area. The secretary of the Jamestown colony wrote that the people they were searching for were those who "escaped from the slaughter of Powhaton of Roanocke." The term *Powhatan* could refer to any Indian leader.

Whatever the true fate or fates of the lost colonists may have been, it seems clear that someone wanted their enterprise to fail—someone who instructed the sailing master, Fernandes, to make things difficult for them, someone who for three years prevented John White from going to their rescue.

One possibility is the Earl of Essex, who was determined to replace Raleigh as the queen's favorite. He could well have contributed to the colony's downfall in the hope of ruining his rival. If so, he nearly succeeded. The expense of outfitting the company and attempting to find it caused Raleigh to complain, "I have consumed the best part of my fortune."

Another likely suspect is Sir Francis Walsingham, Queen Elizabeth's secretary of state. According to author Lee Miller, Walsingham wanted the patent to colonize Virginia for himself, and so did all he could—perhaps with the help of Essex, who was Walsingham's son-in-law—to sabotage Raleigh's enterprise. (For more on Raleigh, Essex, and Walsingham, see the chapter on Christopher Marlowe in the volume in this series titled *Debatable Deaths.*)

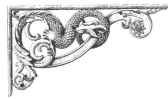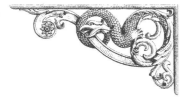

The SALEM WITCH TRIALS

AFTER STRUGGLING TO SURVIVE FOR NEARLY two decades, the Jamestown settlement finally prospered, thanks mainly to the tobacco trade. Encouraged by the Virginians' example, other companies began to establish colonies in the New World. One of the most successful was the Massachusetts Bay Colony, which, between 1629 and 1642, attracted some 16,000 settlers.

Like the colonists of Roanoke and Jamestown, the New Englanders had to cope with crop failures and hostile Indians. But the most insidious threat they faced was one they brought with them from Europe—an ancient superstition that flourished in the religious climate of New England and grew into a sort of mass hysteria that destroyed the lives of hundreds of innocent people.

Belief in witchcraft is almost as old as humankind. The

Opposite:
Massachusetts law defined witchcraft as a "fellowship covenant with a familiar spirit to be punished by death."

21

notion that witches were in league with the devil arose in Europe during the Middle Ages. It wasn't until the sixteenth century, though, that alleged witches were persecuted on a large scale.

In 1542, the English parliament made the practice of witchcraft a crime punishable by death. Over the next century, government-sanctioned witch hunts were common, reaching a peak in the 1640s. An English chronicler wrote in 1646 that in the counties of Essex and Suffolk alone "there were above two hundred indicted within these two years, and above the half of them executed." After that, the witch-hunting frenzy began to subside in Europe.

Across the sea in the Colonies, it was just getting started. From 1647 to 1663, seventy-nine New Englanders were accused of *maleficium*—harming others by supernatural means. Fifteen were hanged. Most of the accused were female; women were thought to be weaker than men, and more likely to succumb to the devil's influence.

Then the number of cases abruptly declined. In the three decades that followed, only four people were convicted of witchcraft, and only one was executed. But in 1692, in the words of historian Carol F. Karlsen, "Satan returned with a vengeance."

The trouble began in the household of Samuel Parris, a Puritan minister who lived in Salem Village (now Danvers), about fifteen miles north of Boston. The village, which wasn't as prosperous as nearby Salem Town, couldn't raise enough tax money to pay Parris's salary. The minister took it personally, hinting in his sermons that the forces of Satan were conspiring against him.

Sometime in the winter of 1691–1692, Parris's nine-year-old daughter, Betty, and her cousin Abigail began displaying bizarre physical symptoms. They seemed "bitten and pinched by invisible agents; their arms, necks, and backs turned this way and that . . . beyond the power of any Epileptick Fits, or natural Disease to effect." By February, two of the girls' friends were having similar episodes.

The families summoned a doctor, who concluded that the girls were bewitched. Under pressure to identify their tormenters, the girls finally fingered three local women, all of them held in low esteem by the community: Sarah Good, a sharp-tongued woman who survived by begging door to door; Tituba, the Parris family's Native American slave; and Sarah Osborne, who failed to attend church regularly.

When they were brought before the local magistrates, Good and Osborne protested their innocence, in vain. Tituba tried a different tactic; she told the authorities what they wanted to hear. She regaled them with elaborate tales of how she and the two Sarahs had flown on broomsticks to Boston, where they joined a coven of witches and "the

When the girls' strange behavior began, Samuel Parris declared, "The Devil hath been raised amongst us," and instructed the citizens of Salem to fast and repent their sins.

Tituba, who grew up on the Caribbean island of Barbados, dabbled in the occult and had a reputation for practicing beneficial, or "white," magic.

devil came to me and bid me serve him."

Tituba's testimony fueled the Puritans' fantasies of a Satanic plot. New accusers came forward, some of them "possessed" like the girls, some not. To the magistrates' alarm, they named not only the village's acknowledged misfits, but some respected citizens as well, including Rebecca Nurse, a devout elderly woman.

It seemed that no accusation was too far-fetched to be taken seriously. Sarah Good's five-year-old daughter, Dorcas, was arrested and imprisoned in chains for several months. After eighteen-year-old Mary Lacey was accused, she began showing signs of "possession" herself. She ended up indicting her own mother and grandmother.

By the end of May, some seventy-five alleged witches had been arrested. Among them were several men—and several people from outside of Salem Village. The effects of the hysteria had begun to spread.

The trials began in June. On June 10, the first condemned witch was hanged. Five more, including Rebecca Nurse and Sarah Good, went to the gallows on July 19. Good shouted at the minister, "I am no more a witch than you are a wizard; and, if you take away my life, God will give you blood to drink!" Legend has it that, years later, the minister suffered an internal hemorrhage and choked to death on his own blood.

On August 19, four men and one woman were hanged. Since those being executed were, for the most part, the ones who declared their innocence most strongly, the accused began pleading guilty—concocting, like Tituba, detailed accounts of how they were recruited by the devil. Most who "confessed" were spared.

Although a few brave souls had protested the witch hunts from the beginning, it wasn't until the wife of the governor and the mother-in-law of the sheriff were accused that the authorities themselves began to question the proceedings.

Eight more died on September 22—the last ever to be executed for witchcraft in Massachusetts. Two weeks later the governor pardoned all the condemned. In April 1693, he released the remaining prisoners. It was too late for Sarah Osborne, who had died in jail, and for little Dorcas Good, who never quite recovered from the experience. Many of the victims retracted their confessions, including Tituba, who said that "her Master did beat

Authorities tried to force Giles Corey to confess by stretching him out on the ground and placing rocks on him. The 81-year-old withstood the increasing weight for two days before he died.

Some claimed that a birthmark or other physical imperfection was a sure sign that a person was a witch. One man was accused simply because he had a large nose.

her and otherways abuse her, to make her confess and accuse . . . her Sister-Witches."

Were the Salem trials merely a case of religious fervor gone wild? Or were there other motives at work? The number of theories may well surpass the number of people hanged. Some historians say that Betty Parris and the others were faking their symptoms, perhaps because they relished the attention it got them.

Others point out that "possession" is a well-known phenomenon that often has nothing to do with witchcraft; Carol Karlsen calls it "a special, altered state of consciousness which some women enter as an involuntary reaction to profound emotional conflict." It's certainly true that the 1690s were a traumatic time. The colonists suffered drought, epidemics, economic troubles, and, worst of all, the French and Indian Wars. Many of the afflicted girls had lost one or both parents in Indian attacks.

It's also been suggested that the girls' strange fits could have been caused by eating grains contaminated with ergot, a fungal plant disease. The symptoms of ergot poisoning include convulsions and hallucinations.

More often, though, scholars place the blame not on nature but on *human* nature. As one author puts it, "Most of the accusations stemmed from revenge, jealousy and greed." The witch hunt may have been, at least in the beginning, an extension of an existing feud between two families: the Putnams, who were supporters of Samuel Parris, and the Porters, who were trying to replace him. Ann Putnam was one of the "possessed" girls; a number of the accused were members of the Porter family.

The authorities themselves also had much to gain from the arrests and executions. All property belonging to the accused was seized by the sheriff, supposedly to cover court costs; very little of it was ever returned.

It's also worth noting that a large percentage of the victims were women who had inherited, or stood to inherit, substantial amounts of money or property. Since estates were traditionally passed on to *male* members of the family, the community may have seen such women as a threat to the established order, and the witch hunts as a way of setting things right.

Samuel Sewall was the only one of the witch trial judges to publicly admit that the death sentences they imposed were wrong.

The MARY CELESTE

THE OCEANS PLAY A LARGE PART IN MANY OF the world's unsolved mysteries, from the extinction of prehistoric species to the lost colony to the Bermuda Triangle, where thousands of planes and ships are said to have vanished without a trace.

The most enigmatic and enduring of maritime mysteries, though, unfolded far from Bermuda and long before anyone had heard of the infamous Triangle. One scholar calls the case of the *Mary Celeste* "a detective-story writer's nightmare: the perfectly perplexing situation without any logical solution—a plot which can never be convincingly unravelled."

The ship seemed ill-fated almost from the day it was launched in May 1861. Originally christened *Amazon*, it was what's known as a brigantine, or half-brig, with square

Opposite: The *Mary Celeste* was spotted floating at sea, an abandoned ship. Abandoned ships weren't an unusual phenomenon in the 1800s. Hundreds were discovered each year. Ordinarily, though, their crews didn't disappear.

Two days before the *Mary Celeste* sailed, Captain Briggs wrote to his mother, "Our vessel is in beautiful trim and I hope we shall have a fine passage."

sails on the foremast and fore-and-aft sails (the sort you see on a sailboat) on the mainmast. As it was about to depart on its first voyage, from Nova Scotia to London, the captain came down with pneumonia and died.

A new captain got the brigantine safely to London but, as he was leaving, he rammed an English ship and sank it. In the fall of 1867, the *Amazon* was wrecked in a gale. It was bought and repaired by an American captain who renamed it *Mary Celeste*. He promptly went bankrupt. The ship was sold to a group of men that included Captain Benjamin Briggs.

Briggs had commanded three other ships and, according to those who knew him, "always bore a good character as a Christian and as an intelligent and active shipmaster." On November 7, 1872, he sailed the *Mary Celeste* out of New York, bound for Genoa, Italy, with 1,700 barrels of denatured alcohol. Also aboard were Briggs's wife, Sarah, their two-year-old daughter, Sophia, and a crew of seven, all considered "peaceable and first-class sailors."

A week later the brigantine *Dei Gratia*—captained by David Morehouse, an old friend of Briggs—also left New York, headed for the British territory of Gibraltar. On December 5, the crew of the *Dei Gratia* sighted a vessel that was "under very short canvas, steering very wild and evidently in distress." Morehouse identified it as the *Mary*

ENIGMATIC EVENTS

Celeste. There was no one at the wheel or anywhere else above decks.

His first mate, Oliver Deveau, boarded her. There was no sign of the captain, his family, or crew. Some of the sails and rigging had blown away. Two of the hatches were open, and several feet of water had collected in the hold. Otherwise, the ship and its cargo were in good shape. The only items missing were some navigational instruments and books, the cargo documents, and one of the yawls, or small boats. It seemed clear that the

The *Mary Celeste* should have been sailing southeast, but when the crew of the *Dei Gratia* spotted her, she was headed in the opposite direction.

crew had abandoned ship hastily. Why they would do so wasn't clear at all.

The last entry in the log was dated ten days earlier: "At five o'clock made island of St Mary's"—an island in the Azores, nearly 400 miles from where the *Mary Celeste* was found. Also on the log slate was a curious message, probably written by the first mate: "Francis my own dear wife, Francis N.R."

There were several other cryptic clues. Under the captain's bunk was a sword with brownish stains on the blade. More dark spots were found on one of the deck rails, plus "a mark of a blow, apparently of a sharp axe." Most puzzling of all, "on either side of the bows of the ship . . . a narrow strip had been cut away." The two grooves, which were about an inch wide and six or seven feet long, seemed to have "been effected intentionally by a sharp instrument."

Sophia Briggs celebrated her second birthday a week before she and her family set off on their ill-fated voyage.

Deveau and two others sailed the *Mary Celeste* to Gibraltar, expecting a substantial reward for salvaging the ship and cargo. But first an inquiry had to be conducted by the British Vice-Admiralty Court.

The attorney general, Solly Flood, seemed determined from the outset to prove that there had been foul play. According to his theory, "the crew got at the alcohol, and in the fury of drunkenness murdered the Master . . . his wife and child and the

ENIGMATIC EVENTS

chief mate," then abandoned the ship. But if the crew members really were drunk, it wasn't from the commercial alcohol in the hold; the additives it contained would have made them deathly ill.

Convinced that the spots on the sword and the rail were bloodstains, Flood gave samples to a local doctor for analysis. The tests showed no trace of blood.

Flood then accused Captain Morehouse of conspiring with his friend Briggs, making it seem as though the *Mary Celeste* had been abandoned, then salvaging and selling the ship and its cargo and splitting the profits. That made little sense, either, since Briggs was part owner of the vessel and would have lost his investment. Unable to pin anything on Morehouse and his crew, the court awarded them 1,700 pounds—only about a fifth of what the ship and its cargo were worth.

Captain Briggs left his son, Arthur, at home. The boy didn't learn of his family's fate until months after the ship was found.

When years went by and there was no word from any of the *Mary Celeste*'s crew, writers began speculating about their fate. Two of the most popular and most reasonable theories: A waterspout blew off the hatch covers and dumped so much water into the hold that the men thought the ship was sinking; or, the barrels of alcohol gave off flammable fumes and, fearing an explosion, they abandoned ship. Both scenarios presume that they climbed into the yawl, which then either drifted off or capsized.

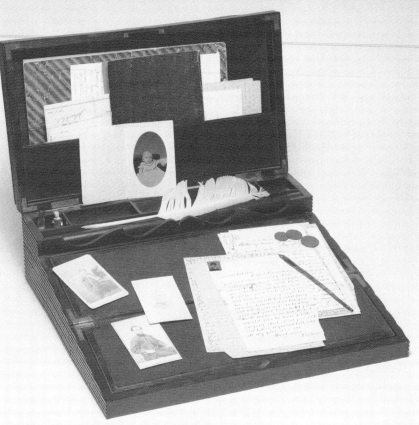

If the crew deliberately abandoned ship, it's unlikely that they would have left behind all their personal belongings. This travel desk, which was found on the ship, belonged to Captain Briggs and held his most prized possessions: letters from his family.

Other theories were harder to buy: The sailors were captured by pirates (what sort of pirate would leave a valuable cargo behind?); they consumed contaminated food or water and, delirious, jumped overboard. And some theories were positively harebrained: A giant octopus dragged everyone aboard (plus the ship's papers and navigational instruments) into the deep; a mysterious island rose from the sea and, when the crew went ashore to explore it, abruptly sank. More recently, it's been proposed that the lot of them were abducted by a UFO.

In the early 1900s, at least four alleged survivors came forward with their own versions of what had happened, none of them very credible. However, one man did provide an intriguing explanation of the odd grooves in the bows: braces were attached there, he said, supporting a small platform that served as a play area for the captain's daughter. When the entire crew crowded onto the platform, it supposedly collapsed, flinging them into the ocean.

We do know for certain what became of the *Mary Celeste*. It was put back into service, changing hands seventeen times in twelve years. One owner swore that "of all the unlucky vessels I ever heard of, she was the most unlucky." A second captain died while commanding the ship. It regularly ran aground, caught fire, or lost part of its cargo. It made its final voyage in 1884; the last owner, who had heavily insured it, deliberately wrecked it on a coral reef off Haiti and burned it in an unsuccessful attempt to collect the insurance money.

The MAINE

BY THE TIME THE *MARY CELESTE* MET ITS END in 1884, the age of sailing ships was ending, too. Ships powered by steam were regularly crossing the ocean, and iron-hulled vessels were beginning to replace wooden ones.

The United States Navy had let its fleet lag far behind those of other industrialized nations. In 1886, it tried to close the gap by authorizing construction of two armored battleships, the *Texas* and the *Maine*. The ships were quickly surpassed by bigger, more modern vessels, and the *Texas* was largely forgotten. The *Maine*, however, soon became a household name throughout America—not because of the battles it won, but because it and most of its crew were destroyed without a fight.

Like the *Mary Celeste,* the *Maine* had a troubled career from the start. While it was still under construction, it

Opposite: "The destruction of that noble vessel," said President McKinley of the battleship *Maine,* "has filled the national heart with inexpressible horror."

This 1898 Currier and Ives lithograph shows the *Maine* as it looked before the explosion.

caught fire; in 1896, it ran aground; the following year, five crewmen were washed overboard; two days later, a shell exploded, injuring two more men; while making its way through New York Harbor, it narrowly missed colliding with an excursion boat, plowing into a pier instead. One thing the battleship hadn't done was fight a battle. The United States was not at war with anyone. But that was about to change.

In 1868, and again in 1895, Cuban nationalists rebelled against Spain, which had controlled Cuba for nearly four centuries. In retaliation, the Spanish army confined most of the island's rural population in concentration camps, where many of the farmers and their families died from disease and starvation.

The United States was drawn into the conflict partly because the American public sympathized with the rebels and partly because American businesses had interests on the island. Officially, the United States government remained neutral; unofficially it began preparing for war.

In January 1898, riots broke out in Havana. Soon afterward, the *Maine,* stationed in Key West, Florida, was ordered to the Cuban capital on what was termed a "friendly call" but was recognized by both sides as a show of strength. A Spanish circular distributed throughout Havana railed against "these Yankee pigs who meddle in our affairs, humiliating us to the last degree, and, for a still greater taunt, order to us a man-of-war of their rotten squadron . . . Death to the Americans!"

Another contemporary lithograph dramatically depicts the disaster.

There were no open acts of hostility, though. For three weeks the *Maine* sat quietly in the harbor. Then, after dark on February 15, the peace was shattered. Clara Barton, head of the American Red Cross, who was in Cuba to aid the *reconcentrados*—the prisoners in the concentration camps—heard "such a burst of thunder as perhaps one never heard before." The *Maine* had been ripped apart by an explosion. A second roar followed, as the ship's forward ammunition magazine detonated. "The air was filled with a blaze of light, and . . . with black specks like huge specters flying in all directions."

The explosion occurred directly under the crew's sleeping quarters. Of the ship's 354 officers and enlisted men, 266 were killed—"crushed by timbers, cut by iron, scorched by fire, and blown sometimes high in the air." Most of the bodies were trapped in the wreckage as the *Maine* sank to the bottom of the harbor; only a portion of its mangled superstructure remained above water.

NAVAL OFFICERS THINK THE MAINE WAS DESTROYED BY A SPANISH MINE.

The commander, Captain Charles Sigsbee, escaped uninjured. Although he suspected that an underwater mine—planted, perhaps, before the ship arrived—had caused the explosion, the message he sent to Washington advised, "Public opinion should be suspended until further report."

But American newspapers did their best to stir up the public. William Randolph Hearst, owner of the *New York Journal,* told his editor, "Please spread the story all over the [front] page. This means war!" A headline in the *New York World* read, "*Maine* explosion caused by bomb or torpedo?" People began sporting buttons with the slogan "Remember the *Maine.*"

President McKinley remained cautious. "The country can afford to withhold its judgment," he said, "and not strike an avenging blow until the truth is known"—to which Assistant Secretary of the Navy Theodore Roosevelt responded, "The president has no more backbone than a chocolate eclair."

Four days after the tragedy, American divers arrived to inspect the wreckage. On February 21, a court of inquiry

When Hearst offered a huge reward to anyone who could identify "the Perpetrator of the Maine Outrage," he was assuming that a Spanish mine was responsible.

began interviewing surviving crew members and naval experts. It concluded that "the *Maine* was destroyed by the explosion of a submarine mine." Although the court didn't fix the blame on anyone, war correspondent Trumbull White wrote that "it was impossible to subdue a general belief that in some way Spanish treachery was responsible for the calamity."

On April 19, 1898, Congress passed a resolution recognizing Cuba's independence and authorizing military intervention. The Spanish-American War lasted only 113 days, but for the United States it was, in the words of author G. J. A. O'Toole, "a national rite of passage, transforming a former colony into a world power."

Although Teddy Roosevelt was nearly forty when the Spanish-American War began, he formed a cavalry regiment, the Rough Riders, and became a war hero.

Ten days after the *Maine* disaster, Roosevelt cabled Commodore George Dewey in Hong Kong, ordering him to ready the United States fleet for war.

In 1912, the *Maine* was brought to the surface and examined by a new board of inquiry, which confirmed that it had been damaged by an external explosion. The ship was then towed out to sea and sunk in deep water. But, although the battleship had been laid to rest, doubts about the cause of its destruction had not.

From the beginning there had been those who questioned the Spanish mine theory, pointing out that Spain had no desire to provoke a war. Some suggested that Cuban nationalists had done the deed, as a way of involving the United States in their cause.

John T. Bucknill, an English engineer and mine expert, discounted the possibility of a mine altogether. One large enough to cause such damage, he said, would have been too large to conceal. In addition, the blast would have caved the hull inward in a dome shape; the *Maine*'s hull had taken the shape of an inverted V. Bucknill suggested that the bituminous coal in one of the ship's bunkers could have exploded due to spontaneous combustion, setting off the powder magazine, and that the damage had made the hull collapse inward.

It was a valid theory. In the preceding three years, more than a dozen navy ships had experienced coal bunker fires; two of these fires had nearly blown up ammunition stored nearby. A number of modern scholars, including Admiral Hyman Rickover, agree with Bucknill's conclusions. Historians Peggy and Harold Samuels insist that a mine was responsible. They believe it was planted by the Weylerites, the group of conservative Spanish landowners and military officers that had spread the circulars proclaiming "Death to the Americans!"

The
TUNGUSKA
EVENT

THE TROUBLE WITH EXPLOSIONS LIKE THE ONE
that destroyed the *Maine* is that whatever caused the blast
is destroyed as well. Historians trying to get at the truth
are, in the words of authors John Baxter and Thomas
Atkins, like "detectives trying to solve a baffling crime in
which the murder weapon is irretrievably lost."

Scientists who study the Tunguska event, which took
place ten years after the *Maine* disaster, are faced with a
similar dilemma. The explosion was at least a thousand
times the size of the atomic blast that leveled Hiroshima.
But the object responsible—if it was an object—left no
trace of itself behind.

The disaster occurred in the valley of the Stony
Tunguska River, in a remote, sparsely populated area of
Siberia. In 1908, the only inhabitants—aside from a few

Opposite: One
scholar calls the
Tunguska explosion
"the greatest natural
disaster in Earth's
recorded history."

45

gold miners—were the Tungus (now called the Evenki), a nomadic people who subsisted mainly by hunting, trapping, and herding reindeer.

A Russian newspaper reported that, around 7:00 a.m. on June 30, villagers in Kenzma, 130 miles from ground zero, saw "a heavenly body of a fiery appearance cut across the sky. . . . When the flying object touched the horizon, a huge flame shot up that cut the sky in two. . . . A noise as from a strong wind was heard, followed immediately by a fearful crash." In another village, the people "ran out into the street in panic. The old women wept and everyone thought the end of the world was approaching."

At the trading station of Vanavara, forty miles from the blast site, a man named S. B. Semenov was knocked off his feet by "a hot wind, as from a cannon." The heat was so intense, he said, that "my shirt almost burned off my back." Nearer to the site, over a thousand reindeer were scorched to death.

The effects of the explosion were felt well beyond Siberia. The seismic waves it generated were recorded all over Europe. The dust and smoke it sent up caused strange atmospheric effects for days afterward. As far away as Spain, people observed "remarkable lights" in the night sky. In London they were so bright that, even at midnight, "it was possible to read large print indoors."

The Europeans didn't connect these phenomena to the Tunguska explosion, because they hadn't heard about it. It wasn't even widely reported within Russia; the country, which was in political turmoil following the revolution of 1905, had more pressing concerns. Those few scientists who knew of the event assumed that an unusually large meteorite had fallen to Earth.

It wasn't until 1928 that the Russian Academy of Sciences sent mineralogist Leonid Kulik to Siberia to find the supposed meteorite. Kulik had trouble getting anyone to lead him to the site. Some of the Tungus believed that the fiery body had been sent by the god Ogdy, and that the place where it fell was sacred.

Finally, with the help of one local man, he located what he called "the cauldron." There was no impact crater, only a huge circle of scorched and flattened forest covering twelve hundred square miles. From the way the fallen trees

Kulik wrote that the extent of the devastation "exceeded all the tales of the eyewitnesses and my wildest expectations."

were fanned out, it was clear where the center of the explosion had been. Even the ground "heaved outward from the spot in giant waves." But in the center itself was a zone where the trees, though stripped of their bark and limbs, were still standing.

There was no sign of a meteorite. Kulik guessed that it had broken up on impact. The following year he returned to search for fragments. He found none. When two more trips failed to turn up any, either, Kulik's colleague E. L. Krinov (who lost a toe to frostbite on the 1929 expedition) suggested that "the meteorite did not explode on the surface of the ground, but in the air."

Astronomers F. J. W. Whipple and I. S. Astapovich came to the same conclusion. But they believed that the object, rather than being solid, like a meteorite or asteroid, was an aggregate of dust, rocks, and ice—in short, a comet. The debate between the pro-comet faction and those who are pro-meteorite has gone on ever since. One science writer calls the controversy "a mere quibble." After all, the two sides agree on the most important point: the Tunguska event was caused by an object from space.

However, as geologist Charles Frankel points out, "science is not a democracy." The fact that something is accepted by the majority doesn't necessarily make it right. Scholars willing to swim against the mainstream have offered some very interesting alternative ideas.

As early as 1941, there was speculation that what struck the earth at Tunguska was not an ordinary object from

Observatories keep a record of all comets that pass near the earth, and no comet was sighted that could have been responsible for the Tunguska event.

space, but one composed of antimatter—a hypothetical form of matter made up of particles whose electrical charge is opposite to that of normal matter. According to Nobel Prize-winning chemist Willard Libby, a chunk of antimatter might pass through Earth's upper atmosphere intact, but the denser lower atmosphere "might heat it to the gaseous stage and dissemble it explosively."

After the atomic bomb was dropped on Hiroshima in 1945, Russian engineer Aleksander Kazantsev noted how similar the blast damage was to that in Kulik's "cauldron." Assuming that the Tunguska event was also a nuclear explosion, Kazantsev imagined a scenario in which an alien spaceship blew up while hovering over Siberia.

Another science-fictionish theory, proposed by physi-

A transformer built by Tesla in 1900 produced "lightning bolts" of ten to twelve million volts. They knocked out the local power company's generator and created thunder that could be heard fifteen miles away.

cists A. A. Jackson and Michael P. Ryan, has the earth being pierced by a miniature black hole—an ultradense form of matter created by a collapsed star. Yet another hypothesis is that a laser beam was sent our way as a signal (or perhaps a warning?) by beings on another planet; if so, it certainly got our attention.

Not long before the Tunguska event, the noted inventor Nikola Tesla had begun experimenting with high-voltage electricity. Tesla hoped to create an "intelligent machine" that would use the earth itself as a conductor "to transmit power, in unlimited amounts to any terrestrial distance." If it were used as a weapon, he said, it could "destroy any-thing . . . within a radius of 200 miles." Some wonder whether, in June 1908, Tesla might have been giving the device a test run.

In 2002, Russian geologist Vladimir Epifanov attacked the problem from a whole new direction—from underground. The Tunguska site lies above a large reservoir of natural gas. Epifanov claims that, if an earthquake opened up a fissure, a jet of gas could have shot out, been ignited by electricity in the upper atmosphere, then plunged back to Earth in the form of a huge fireball that, when supplied with oxygen, exploded.

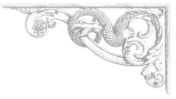

The HINDENBURG

ONE OF THE MOST BAFFLING THINGS ABOUT
the German airship *Hindenburg* is the fact that it's so
famous. Since it went down in flames in 1937, it's become
a universally recognized symbol, second only to the *Titanic*,
of how the grandest, most ambitious plans can come to a
miserable end.

According to author Michael Mooney, the destruction
of the *Hindenburg* was perhaps "the most completely documented, reported, and analyzed disaster on record." Yet,
as air disasters go, it wasn't all that catastrophic. Thirty-six
passengers and crew were killed. But twice that number
lost their lives when the American dirigible *Akron* crashed
at sea in 1933—an event that's all but forgotten.

The *Hindenburg*'s notoriety, like that of the dinosaurs,
may have something to do with its sheer size: at over eight

Opposite: Several
witnesses compared
the glowing airship
to a huge Japanese
lantern, but one man
thought it looked
more like "a scene
from a medieval
picture of hell."

53

hundred feet in length, it was the largest aircraft ever built. Or its fame may be due to the fact that so many spectators, reporters, and photographers witnessed its demise. Or maybe we consider the disaster so significant because it affected far more than just a single airship—it destroyed the whole future of lighter-than-air travel.

One thing is certain: the *Hindenburg* doesn't owe its immortality to some impenetrable mystery like the one surrounding that other doomed ship, the *Mary Celeste.* After all, the cause of the disaster is common knowledge: the hydrogen in the cells of the airship was set afire by an electrical spark. But, as I've mentioned before in this series, common knowledge is not the same as fact—and the facts have led some researchers to very different conclusions.

Although it sailed the sky and not the sea, the

Hindenburg had one thing in common with the *Mary Celeste* and the *Maine:* from the time of its construction, it seemed cursed by bad luck. Much of the duralumin—a light, strong aluminum alloy—that was used in its frame came from a British airship that crashed in 1930, killing most of those on board.

When construction was completed and the *Hindenburg* was being taken from its hangar, a gust of wind caught it and damaged one of the tail fins. On its first commercial flight, one of its engines failed; a second engine gave out on the way back to Germany. But after making ten uneventful trips to the United States in 1936, the ship was pronounced completely safe. An American reporter declared that "only a stroke of war or an unfathomable Act of God will ever mar this German dirigible passenger safety record."

The crew didn't consider the hydrogen—which makes an explosive mixture when combined with oxygen—a particular problem. Other German airships had been struck by bullets, lightning, even antiaircraft shells, without catching fire. The gas cells were designed to be leakproof, metal catwalks and ladders were covered with rubber to prevent sparks, and the use of matches

Riding in the giant airship was so comfortable that one 85-year-old passenger declared, "It was too boring. You can't even feel seasick."

was limited to a single sealed room. The designers had hoped to use helium, a non-flammable gas, but the United States controlled most of the world's supply of helium and refused to sell any to Germany.

"How do I know," asked the secretary of the interior, "that it won't ultimately be used for war purposes?" It was a legitimate concern; Adolf Hitler had come to power in 1933 and was building up the country's armed forces. His advisers saw the *Hindenburg* as an instrument of propaganda, proof of Germany's technological superiority, and ordered a huge swastika, the symbol of the Nazi Party, painted on the tail fins.

Many Americans found the dirigible fascinating. While the *Hindenburg* was moored at the Naval Air Station in Lakehurst, New Jersey, in 1936, it drew over 100,000 visitors. But the ship and its swastika also inspired anti-Nazi demonstrations and threats of violence.

There had been attempts in the past to sabotage German airships. Bombs were found aboard the *Bodensee,* the *Nordstern,* and the *Graf Zeppelin.* Before the *Hindenburg's* first flight of the 1937 season, Dr. Hugo Eckener, the craft's designer, "repeatedly received anonymous letters warning the *Hindenburg* not to land at Lakehurst." The German ambassador to the United States got similar letters, including one from a Milwaukee woman who warned, "The Zeppelin [dirigible] is going to be destroyed by a time bomb during its flight to another country. Please believe my words as the truth, so that no one later will have cause for regret."

German security police examined the luggage and mail and combed the *Hindenburg* with a portable X-ray machine but found no trace of what they called an "infernal device." Soon after the ship left Germany on May 3, it ran into a headwind that slowed its progress. It didn't reach Lakehurst until late afternoon on May 6. A thunderstorm had just passed over; there were flashes of lightning on the horizon, and a light drizzle was falling.

The dirigible approached the mooring mast; lines were tossed to the ground crew. Then, wrote a *New York Times* reporter, "those on the ground heard a low report or boom from the ship. Almost simultaneously there was a flash which lighted up the twilight, and sent a thrill of terror through the onlookers. This was followed quickly by the bursting of flames from the rear gondola [passenger compartment] . . . the flames spread forward, and in a moment the gigantic ship seemed to be enveloped in fire."

Incredibly, most of the ninety-seven passengers and crew got out alive. As

At first, some spectators mistook the flames for fireworks.

As the airship fell, it broke in two, and flames spurted from the nose. One reporter called the disaster "a moment of spectacular madness."

the burning airship sank toward the earth, some broke windows and leaped out. After the gondola struck the ground, others stumbled, unharmed, from the inferno. The fourteen-year-old cabin boy, trapped in the flaming wreckage, survived only because a water tank above him burst, soaking him.

A week after the disaster, Dr. Eckener, the ship's designer, visited the site. "It appeared to me," he later wrote, "the hopeless end of a great dream." He was right. Although blimps—smaller craft without a rigid frame— went on flying, the age of the great airships ended with the burning of the *Hindenburg.*

No one seemed quite certain what had caused the conflagration. There was no shortage of theories, though: lightning, sparks from the engine exhaust, static electricity from the mooring lines, a loose propeller. An inventor from Connecticut claimed that an experimental rocket he set off that evening had traveled all the way to New Jersey and accidentally struck the airship.

Many of the officers and crew suspected that the destruction was deliberate. Ernst Lehmann, an airship captain who was aboard as a passenger, believed "it must have been an infernal machine [a bomb]." So did Dr. Eckener. Later, under pressure from the German Air Ministry, Eckener retracted this opinion. Both German and American officials feared that "a finding of sabotage might be cause for an international incident."

A board of inquiry made up of representatives from

both countries concluded that "there was a small amount of explosive mixture [hydrogen and oxygen] in the upper part of the ship through a leak in a gas cell" and that it "could have been ignited by St. Elmo's fire or a similar electric phenomenon." Saint Elmo's fire is a high-voltage electrical field produced during storms; it appears as a glowing halo atop tall structures and on the wings of airplanes. Two witnesses later recalled seeing a blue flame flickering about the *Hindenburg* just before it caught fire.

The *Hindenburg* explosion marked the first time that photographers and journalists were at the scene of a major disaster.

But inside the ship, the chief engineer, Rudolf Sauter, had seen something quite different: a bright burst of light accompanied by a low popping sound, like a flashbulb going off. It occurred in the middle of one of the gas cells, at the point where a catwalk passed through it. Sauter was convinced that someone had planted an incendiary device.

In the blackened, twisted wreckage, the New York Police Department bomb squad discovered what was identified as "the insoluble residue from . . . a small dry battery." Author A. A. Hoehling, who interviewed members of the *Hindenburg*'s crew, suggests that the battery, along with a

Not everyone could afford a ticket on the *Hindenburg*. A one-way trip cost $400—a lot of money in 1937.

timer, could have been used to set off a flashbulb, producing enough heat and enough oxygen to ignite the hydrogen.

Such a device could have been installed only by someone with access to restricted areas of the airship. Both Hoehling and Michael Mooney put the blame on Eric Spehl, one of the ship's riggers. Spehl was dating a woman with ties to Communists and other revolutionaries who were violently opposed to the sorts of fascist regimes that controlled Italy and Germany. She could well have convinced him that sabotaging the airship would be striking a blow against the Nazis. There's one other fact that makes Spehl a prime suspect: he was an amateur photographer who sometimes brought camera equipment on board.

In the 1990s, retired NASA engineer Adison Bain discovered evidence that the *Hindenburg* fire was fueled by more than just hydrogen and oxygen. Bain analyzed a surviving scrap of the airship's fabric covering and found that it was coated with a variety of flammable compounds, including cellulose nitrate and aluminum powder—one of the ingredients in rocket fuel. When he zapped the fabric with 30,000 volts of electricity, "Poof, it disappeared. . . . I guess the moral of the story is, don't paint your airship with rocket fuel."

ENIGMATIC EVENTS

WORDS FOR THE WISE

anthropologist A scientist who studies human social life, culture, and origins.

Armada A fleet of ships sent by Spain's King Philip II to invade England in 1588. Its defeat by the English was one of the decisive battles in European history, signaling the rise of Britain as a world power.

asteroid A stony object that orbits the sun but is too small to be considered a planet. Most asteroids are found between Mars and Jupiter, in a swarm called the asteroid belt. The largest, Ceres, has a diameter of about 500 miles.

Barton, Clara (1821–1912) Civil War nurse known as the "Angel of the Battlefield." In 1881 she founded the American Red Cross to aid victims of war and disaster.

Bermuda Triangle An area of the Atlantic Ocean off southeast Florida. Because so many ships and airplanes have disappeared there, some people claim that a mysterious force is at work within the Triangle; others say that the number of planes and ships lost there is no greater than in any other part of the ocean.

black hole A theoretical celestial body created by the collapse of a dead star. Its field of gravity is so strong that no light can escape from it.

comet A low-density celestial body, a sort of "dirty snowball" composed of gas and small particles held together by frozen water, ammonia, methane, and carbon dioxide. When a comet's orbit takes it near the sun, it releases a stream of gas and dust, forming a "tail" that can stretch for millions of miles.

Drake, Sir Francis (about 1541–1596) English seaman who led an expedition that sailed around the world in 1577–1580. Drake also played a major role in the defeat of the Spanish Armada.

Essex, Earl of (1566–1601) Robert Devereux, second Earl of Essex, became the favorite companion of Queen Elizabeth I. After a failed military campaign against Ireland, he fell out of favor. He tried to lead a rebellion against the queen and was beheaded for treason.

fascism A political movement that emerged after World War I in several European countries, including Italy, Germany, and Spain. Fascist regimes, which are typically controlled by a dictator, consider the state more important than the individual.

French and Indian Wars A long and bloody series of conflicts that took place in North America between 1689 and 1763. The hostilities were an extension of larger wars in Europe involving England, France, Austria, and Spain. In the New World, Native Americans were caught up in the conflict, some siding with the French, others with the English.

Hearst, William Randolph (1863–1951) American publisher whose journalistic empire included twenty-five daily newspapers and such well-known magazines as *Good Housekeeping, Cosmopolitan,* and *Harper's Bazaar.* Hearst's papers specialized in the biased, sensational sort of coverage known as "yellow journalism."

Jamestown The first permanent English settlement in North America, established in 1607 on a marshy peninsula on the James River in Virginia. Jamestown survived disease, famine, Indian attacks, and being burned to the ground, only to be replaced by Williamsburg as the seat of Virginia's government in 1699.

McKinley, William (1843–1901) President of the United States from 1897 until 1901, when he was shot to death by an anarchist. McKinley was succeeded by his vice president and former assistant secretary of the navy, Theodore Roosevelt.

meteor An interplanetary body, composed of stone or iron or both, that burns up in the earth's atmosphere, creating the streak of light we call a shooting star or falling star. Before the object hits our atmosphere, it's technically known as a meteoroid. If some of the meteor survives and strikes the earth, it's called a meteorite.

mine An explosive device equipped with one or more triggers that set off a charge when they come into contact with a ship, a vehicle, or a person.

Nazi Party A German political party whose major tenets included an extreme nationalism and a belief in the superiority of the German "race" that led to the execution of millions of Jews, as well as homosexuals and Gypsies.

paleontologist A scientist who studies fossils.

Spanish-American War (1898) A brief but bloody conflict that began with America supporting Cuba's independence from Spain and ended with Spain handing over control of Puerto Rico, Guam, and the Philippine Islands to the United States. Although fewer than four hundred Americans died in battle, thousands were killed by tropical diseases and contaminated food.

spontaneous combustion A process of oxidation that slowly raises the heat of combustible materials—such as coal, moist hay, and rags soaked with oil or paint—until they burst into flame.

Tesla, Nikola (1856–1943) Croatian-American inventor who developed a practical electrical motor that produced alternating current.

waterspout A funnel cloud, similar to a tornado, that occurs over the ocean in tropical areas. The water in the funnel consists mainly of condensed vapor from the air.

TO LEARN MORE ABOUT
ENIGMATIC EVENTS

BOOKS
Nonfiction

Bosco, Peter I. *Roanoke: The Story of the Lost Colony*. Spotlight
on American History series. Brookfield, CT: Millbrook, 1992.
A brief but accurate account of the Roanoke settlement that
focuses on John White and scientist Thomas Hariot, but also
includes information about the Native Americans and their
way of life.

Gallant, Roy A. *The Day the Sky Split Apart: Investigating a
Cosmic Mystery*. New York: Simon & Schuster, 1995.
Gallant, sometimes called "the Indiana Jones of astronomers,"
visited the site of the Tunguska explosion and writes about it
with authority. His prose is both scientific in tone and readable.

Jackson, Shirley. *The Witchcraft of Salem Village*. Landmark
Books series. New York: Random House, 1987.
This well-written narrative of the Salem witch trials is consid-
ered the definitive book on the subject for young readers.

Marrin, Albert. *The Spanish-American War*. New York:
Atheneum, 1991.
An in-depth history of the conflict and its causes.

Fiction

Majoor, Mireille. *Inside the Hindenburg*. New York: Little, Brown, 2000.
Although this book centers around a fictional story involving
two young passengers on the airship, Ken Marschall's illustrations are the main attraction—detailed, technically accurate
paintings of all areas of the craft.

Speare, Elizabeth George. *The Witch of Blackbird Pond*. Boston: Houghton Mifflin, 2001.

This Newbery Medal winner takes place in Connecticut at the time of the witchcraft scare.

ONLINE INFORMATION

www.galisteo.com/scripts/tngscript/default.prl

Good photos of the Tunguska event site, links to other Web sites, bulletin board.

www.nationalgeographic.com/features/97/salem

An interactive Web site that lets you "experience" the Salem witch trials by becoming one of the accused and making choices.

www.salemwitchmuseum.com

Features a brief overview of the witch trials, a virtual tour of sites related to the trials, and an online store.

OUTDOOR DRAMA

The Lost Colony.

This history-based drama with music has been performed on Roanoke Island annually since 1937. Runs from June through August. For more information, go to www.thelostcolony.org

BIBLIOGRAPHY

Aron, Paul. *Unsolved Mysteries of American History: An Eye-Opening Journey through 500 Years of Discoveries, Disappearances, and Baffling Events.* New York: Wiley, 1997.

Bakker, Robert T., PhD. *The Dinosaur Heresies: New Theories Unlocking the Mystery of the Dinosaurs and Their Extinction.* New York: Morrow, 1986.

Baldwin, Hanson W. *Sea Fights and Shipwrecks: True Tales of the Seven Seas.* Garden City, NY: Hanover House, 1955.

Baxter, John, and Thomas Atkins. *The Fire Came By: The Riddle of the Great Siberian Explosion.* Garden City, NY: Doubleday, 1976.

Botting, Douglas, and the Editors of Time-Life Books. *The Giant Airships.* Alexandria, VA: Time-Life, 1981.

Breslaw, Elaine G. *Tituba, Reluctant Witch of Salem: Devilish Indians and Puritan Fantasies.* New York: New York University Press, 1996.

Cheney, Margaret. *Tesla: Man Out of Time.* Englewood Cliffs, NJ: Prentice-Hall, 1981.

"Deep Impact: New Hypothesis of the Tunguska Explosion." www.spacedaily.com/news/deepimpact-02q.html

DiChristina, Mariette. "What Really Downed the *Hindenburg.*" www.ch2bc.org/hindenburg.htm

Durant, David N. *Ralegh's Lost Colony: The Story of the First English Settlement in America.* New York: Atheneum, 1981.

Editors of Reader's Digest. *Great Mysteries of the Past: Experts Unravel Fact and Fallacy Behind the Headlines of History.* Pleasantville, NY: Reader's Digest, 1991.

Editors of Reader's Digest. *Mysteries of the Unexplained.* Pleasantville, NY: Reader's Digest, 1982.

Frankel, Charles. *The End of the Dinosaurs: Chicxulub Crater and Mass Extinctions.* Cambridge, England: Cambridge University Press, 1999.

Great Moments of the Century as Reported by The New York Times. New York: Arno Press, 1977.

Hoehling, A. A. *Who Destroyed the* Hindenburg? New York: Popular Library, 1962.

Horner, John R., and Edwin Dobb. *Dinosaur Lives: Unearthing an Evolutionary Saga.* New York: HarperCollins, 1997.

Karlsen, Carol F. *The Devil in the Shape of a Woman: Witchcraft in Colonial New England.* New York: Norton, 1998.

Miller, Lee. *Roanoke: Solving the Mystery of the Lost Colony.* New York: Arcade, 2000.

Mooney, Michael Macdonald. *The Hindenburg.* New York: Dodd, Mead, 1972.

Mysteries of Mind Space & Time: The Unexplained. Vols. 6, 16, 24. Westport, CT: H. S. Stuttman, 1992.

O'Toole, G. J. A. *The Spanish War: An American Epic—1898.* New York: Norton, 1984.

Quinn, David Beers. *Set Fair for Roanoke: Voyages and Colonies, 1584–1606.* Chapel Hill: University of North Carolina Press, 1985.

Rickover, H. G. *How the Battleship* Maine *Was Destroyed*. Washington, DC: Department of the Navy, 1976.

Shermer, Michael, ed. *The* Skeptic *Encyclopedia of Pseudoscience*. Santa Barbara, CA: ABC Clio, 2002.

Spicer, Stanley T. *The Saga of the* Mary Celeste: *Ill-Fated Mystery Ship*. Halifax, NS: Nimbus, 2002.

Stoneley, Jack. *Tunguska: Cauldron of Hell*. London: W. H. Allen, 1977.

Taylor, John M. *The Witchcraft Delusion: The Story of the Witchcraft Persecutions in Seventeenth-Century New England, Including Original Trial Transcripts*. New York: Gramercy, 1995.

"Tesla Wireless and the Tunguska Explosion." www.frank.germano.com/tunguska.htm

Toland, John. *The Great Dirigibles: Their Triumphs and Disasters*. New York: Dover, 1972.

White, Trumbull. *United States in War with Spain and the History of Cuba*. Chicago: International, 1898.

Whitehouse, David. "Mystery Space Blast 'Solved'." news.bbc.co.uk/1/hi/sci/tech/1628806.stm

Wilford, John Noble. *The Riddle of the Dinosaur*. New York: Knopf, 1985.

Yool, George Malcolm. *1692 Witch Hunt: The Layman's Guide to the Salem Witchcraft Trials*. Bowie, MD: Heritage, 1992.

NOTES ON QUOTES

Introduction

Page vi, "the grandest": Bakker, *The Dinosaur Heresies*, p. 38.

Page vii, "One great flaw": Miller, *Roanoke*, p. ix.

Page vii, "the miraculous": Editors of Reader's Digest, *Mysteries of the Unexplained*, p. 8.

Chapter One: The Death of the Dinosaurs

Page 2, "If we measured": Bakker, *The Dinosaur Heresies*, p. 16.

Page 3, "seem to have": Horner and Dobb, *Dinosaur Lives*, p. 207.

Page 4, "like jam": *Mysteries of Mind Space & Time*, vol. 6, p. 698.

Page 5, "the Chicxulub crater": Frankel, *The End of the Dinosaurs*, p. 111.

Page 6, "The mass murder": Bakker, *The Dinosaur Heresies*, p. 425.

Chapter Two: The Lost Colony

Page 13, "most gentle, loving" and "most beautiful": Quinn, *Set Fair for Roanoke,* pp. 37 & 39.

Page 15, "lewdly forsook" and "leaving her distressed": Miller, *Roanoke,* p. 64.

Page 15, "we found none": Durant, *Ralegh's Lost Colony,* p. 114.

Page 16, "earnestly entreated": Miller, *Roanoke,* p. 76.

Page 16, "if they should": Aron, *Unsolved Mysteries of American History,* p. 42.

Page 16, "he would prepare": Miller, *Roanoke,* p. 192.

Page 16, "there is little": ibid., p. 193.

Page 16, "We found the houses": Durant, *Ralegh's Lost Colony,* pp. 148–149.

Page 16, "in fayre Capitall": ibid., p. 149.

Page 17, "thus committing": Miller, *Roanoke,* p. 18.

Page 17, "the parties by him": ibid., p. 207.

Page 17, "A whole country": ibid., p. 211.

Page 18, "miserably slaughtered": Durant, *Ralegh's Lost Colony,* p. 161.

Page 18, "howses built" and "haire of a perfect": Aron, *Unsolved Mysteries of American History,* p. 42.

Page 18, "And thus we left": Miller, *Roanoke,* p. 226.

Page 18, "several of their": ibid., p. 263.

Page 19, "escaped from the slaughter": ibid., p. 233.

Page 19, "I have consumed": ibid., p. 201.

Chapter Three: The Salem Witch Trials

Page 22, "there were above": Taylor, *The Witchcraft Delusion,* p. ix.

Page 22, "Satan returned": Karlsen, *The Devil in the Shape of a Woman,* p. 35.

Page 23, "bitten and pinched": Aron, *Unsolved Mysteries of American History,* p. 52.

Page 23, "the devil came": Breslaw, *Tituba, Reluctant Witch of Salem,* p. 118.

Page 24, "I am no more": Yool, *1692 Witch Hunt,* p. 103.

Page 25, "her Master did": Breslaw, *Tituba, Reluctant Witch of Salem,* p. 172.

Page 26, "a special, altered": Karlsen, *The Devil in the Shape of a Woman,* p. 249.

Page 27, "Most of the accusations": Yool, *1692 Witch Hunt,* p. 1.

Chapter Four: The *Mary Celeste*

Page 29, "a detective-story": *Mysteries of Mind Space & Time,* vol. 16, p. 1881.

Page 30, "always bore": Spicer, *The Saga of the* Mary Celeste, p. 29.

Page 30, "peaceable and first-class": ibid., p. 30.

Page 30, "under very short": ibid., p. 37.

Page 32, "At five o'clock": *Mysteries of Mind Space & Time,* vol. 16, p. 1876.

Page 32, "Francis my own": Baldwin, *Sea Fights and Shipwrecks,* p. 245.

Page 32, "a mark of": ibid., p. 248.

Page 32, "on either side" and "been effected": ibid., p. 250.

Page 32, "the crew got": ibid., p. 253.

Page 35, "of all the unlucky": Spicer, *The Saga of the* Mary Celeste, p. 52.

Chapter Five: The *Maine*

Page 38, "friendly call": Rickover, *How the Battleship* Maine *Was Destroyed,* p. 34.

Page 39, "these Yankee pigs": O'Toole, *The Spanish War,* p. 25.

Page 39, "such a burst" and "The air was filled": ibid., p. 29.

Page 39, "crushed by timbers": ibid., p. 31.

Page 40, "Public opinion should": ibid., p. 33.

Page 40, "Please spread the story": ibid., p. 34.

Page 40, "*Maine* explosion caused": Aron, *Unsolved Mysteries of American History,* p. 117.

Page 40, "The country can": ibid., p. 115.

Page 40, "The president has": ibid., p. 116.

Page 41, "the *Maine* was destroyed": White, *United States in War with Spain and the History of Cuba,* p. 313.

Page 41, "it was impossible": ibid., p. 36.

Page 41, "a national rite": O'Toole, *The Spanish War,* p. 18.

Chapter Six: The Tunguska Event

Page 45, "detectives trying": Baxter and Atkins, *The Fire Came By,* p. 138.

Page 46, "a heavenly body": Stoneley, *Tunguska,* p. 23.

Page 46, "ran out into": ibid., p. 24.

Page 46, "a hot wind": ibid., p. 51.

Page 46, "my shirt almost": Baxter and Atkins, *The Fire Came By,* p. 64.

Page 46, "remarkable lights": ibid., p. 26.

Page 46, "it was possible": ibid., p. 29.

Page 48, "heaved outward": ibid., p. 74.

Page 48, "the meteorite did not": ibid., p. 85.

Page 48, "a mere quibble": Shermer, *The Skeptic Encyclopedia of Pseudoscience,* p. 256.

Page 48, "science is not": Frankel, *The End of the Dinosaurs*, p. 57.

Page 49, "might heat it": Baxter and Atkins, *The Fire Came By*, p. 116.

Page 50, "to transmit power": Cheney, *Tesla: Man Out of Time*, p. 143.

Page 50, "destroy anything": "Tesla Wireless and the Tunguska Explosion," pp. 1–2.

Chapter Seven: The *Hindenburg*

Page 53, "the most completely": Mooney, *The Hindenburg*, p. 270.

Page 55, "only a stroke": Toland, *The Great Dirigibles*, p. 338.

Page 56, "How do I know": Hoehling, *Who Destroyed the* Hindenburg?, p. 7.

Page 56, "repeatedly received": ibid., p. 8.

Page 56, "The Zeppelin": Botting, *The Giant Airships*, p. 154.

Page 57, "those on the ground": *Great Moments of the Century as Reported by* The New York Times, p. 114.

Page 58, "It appeared to me": Botting, *The Giant Airships*, p. 163.

Page 58, "it must have been": Toland, *The Great Dirigibles*, p. 338.

Page 58, "a finding of sabotage": Mooney, *The Hindenburg*, p. 271.

Page 59, "there was a small" and "could have been": Hoehling, *Who Destroyed the* Hindenburg?, p. 169.

Page 59, "the insoluble residue": ibid., p. 173.

Page 60, "Poof, it disappeared": DiChristina, "What Really Downed the *Hindenburg*," p. 4.

INDEX

Page numbers for illustrations are in boldface

ABOUT THE AUTHOR

GARY L. BLACKWOOD has long been fascinated both with history and with the mysterious, so it's only natural that he should combine the two—not only in this set of books but in many of his other works, including the non-fiction series SECRETS OF THE UNEXPLAINED and the historical novels *The Shakespeare Stealer, The Year of the Hangman,* and *Second Sight.*

GEORGE
ARMSTRONG
CUSTER

Other titles in *Historical American Biographies*

Alexander Graham Bell
Inventor and Teacher
ISBN 0-7660-1096-1

Andrew Carnegie
*Steel King and
Friend to Libraries*
ISBN 0-7660-1212-3

Annie Oakley
Legendary Sharpshooter
ISBN 0-7660-1012-0

Benjamin Franklin
*Founding Father and
Inventor*
ISBN 0-89490-784-0

Billy the Kid
Outlaw of the Wild West
ISBN 0-7660-1091-0

Buffalo Bill Cody
Western Legend
ISBN 0-7660-1015-5

Clara Barton
Civil War Nurse
ISBN 0-89490-778-6

Daniel Boone
Frontier Legend
ISBN 0-7660-1256-5

Dolley Madison
Courageous First Lady
ISBN 0-7660-1092-9

George Armstrong Custer
*Civil War General and
Western Legend*
ISBN 0-7660-1255-7

Jane Addams
*Nobel Prize Winner and
Founder of Hull House*
ISBN 0-7660-1094-5

Jeb Stuart
Confederate Cavalry General
ISBN 0-7660-1013-9

Jefferson Davis
President of the Confederacy
ISBN 0-7660-1064-3

Jesse James
Legendary Outlaw
ISBN 0-7660-1055-4

Jim Bowie
Hero of the Alamo
ISBN 0-7660-1253-0

John Wesley Powell
*Explorer of the
Grand Canyon*
ISBN 0-89490-783-2

Lewis and Clark
Explorers of the Northwest
ISBN 0-7660-1016-3

Louisa May Alcott
Author of Little Women
ISBN 0-7660-1254-9

Mark Twain
*Legendary Writer
and Humorist*
ISBN 0-7660-1093-7

Martha Washington
First Lady
ISBN 0-7660-1017-1

Mary Todd Lincoln
*Tragic First Lady
of the Civil War*
ISBN 0-7660-1252-2

Paul Revere
*Rider for the
Revolution*
ISBN 0-89490-779-4

Robert E. Lee
*Southern Hero of the
Civil War*
ISBN 0-89490-782-4

Robert Fulton
*Inventor and
Steamboat Builder*
ISBN 0-7660-1141-0

Stonewall Jackson
Confederate General
ISBN 0-89490-781-6

Susan B. Anthony
*Voice for Women's
Voting Rights*
ISBN 0-89490-780-8

Thomas Alva Edison
Inventor
ISBN 0-7660-1014-7

Thomas Nast
Political Cartoonist
ISBN 0-7660-1251-4

The Wright Brothers
*Inventors of
the Airplane*
ISBN 0-7660-1095-3

Historical American Biographies

GEORGE ARMSTRONG CUSTER

Civil War General and Western Legend

Zachary Kent

Enslow Publishers, Inc.

40 Industrial Road   PO Box 38
Box 398   Aldershot
Berkeley Heights, NJ 07922 Hants GU12 6BP
USA   UK

http://www.enslow.com

Library of Congress Cataloging-in-Publication Data

Kent, Zachary.
    George Armstrong Custer : Civil War General and western legend /
Zachary Kent.
        p. cm. — (Historical American biographies)
    Includes bibliographical references (p.) and index.
    Summary: Traces the life of the legendary Civil War general who began
his career as a West Point cadet and after becoming a legend in the west
was perhaps best-known for his "last stand."
    ISBN 0-7660-1255-7
    1. Custer, George Armstrong, 1839–1876 Juvenile literature.
2. Generals—United States Biography Juvenile literature. 3. United
States. Army Biography Juvenile literature. [1. Custer, George
Armstrong, 1839–1876. 2. Generals.] I. Title. II. Series.
E467.1.C99K38   2000
973.8'2'092
[B]—DC21   99-27496
                                                    CIP

Printed in the United States of America

10 9 8 7 6 5 4 3 2 1

To Our Readers:
All Internet addresses in this book were active and appropriate when we
went to press. Any comments or suggestions can be sent by e-mail to
Comments@enslow.com or to the address on the back cover.

Illustration Credits: Enslow Publishers, Inc., pp. 21, 31, 38, 105;
Library of Congress, pp. 8, 11, 29, 39, 44, 52, 62, 68, 73, 109, 112;
National Archives, pp. 26, 35, 48, 57, 64, 70, 82, 90, 93, 98;
Reproduced from the *Dictionary of American Portraits*, Published by
Dover Publications, Inc., in 1967, pp. 6, 43; United States Military
Archives, p. 18.

Cover Illustration: National Archives (Inset); Corel Corporation
(Background—*Custer's Last Fight*, Artist Unknown).

CONTENTS

George Armstrong Custer

1

THE LITTLE BIGHORN

Six hundred horsemen of the United States 7th Cavalry Regiment trotted across the grassy hills of southeastern Montana in the early morning hours of June 25, 1876. A pack train of 175 mules carried food, supplies, and ammunition. Arikara and Crow scouts scanned the horizon in all directions. At the head of this army column rode thirty-six-year-old Lieutenant Colonel George Armstrong Custer. Tall and muscular, he was dressed in a buckskin coat, his blond hair cut short. *The Detroit Advertiser and Tribune* had once called Custer "a man of tireless energy and iron endurance. Difficulty and hardship only serve to bring out the wonderful qualities he

possesses."[1] An army officer all his adult life, on this summer day Custer was itching for a fight.

From a mountaintop later named the Crow's Nest, Custer's scouts spotted a Sioux and Cheyenne village some fifteen miles away. Scout Mitch Bouyer insisted, "[I]f you don't find more Indians in the valley than you ever saw together, you can hang me."[2]

Custer hurried back to his men and excitedly told the officers, "The largest Indian camp on the North American continent is ahead and I am going to attack it."[3] The size of the village did not concern Custer.

Before the Sioux and Cheyenne could scatter, the 7th Cavalry would have to advance and attack at once. Custer rode among the troops, promising them a victory.

It was just past noon when the cavalry entered the valley and approached the Little

Instead of a regulation blue army coat, Custer preferred to wear a fringed buckskin jacket while serving in the West. Such clothes gave him the look of a hardy frontiersman.

Bighorn River. Here, Custer divided his regiment into four sections. One hundred twenty-five of his troops, commanded by Captain Frederick Benteen, went scouting to the south. Another eighty remained behind to protect the pack train. Major Marcus Reno, with 140 men, was ordered to pursue Sioux warriors who were seen fleeing downriver. Reno was to ride down into the valley, ford the river, and attack the southern end of the village. Custer, with the remaining 225 troopers, would skirt around northwestward and pitch in with a wild charge from the east.

As Reno departed, chief scout Lieutenant Charles Varnum joined Lieutenant Colonel Custer.

"What can you see?" asked Custer.

"The whole valley in front is full of Indians," Varnum reported, pointing to the hill to the north. He said Custer would be able to see the Indians from the hill.[4]

Custer quickly led his 225 men in that direction, over ridges and ravines. When they reached a bluff, Half Yellow Face, a Crow scout who was riding beside Custer, exclaimed, "The Sioux must be running away." Scout Frederick Gerard waved his hat, shouting, "Here are your Indians, running like devils!"[5] From the crest of the bluff, Custer clearly viewed the great Indian village for the first time. It stretched beside the river for three miles. Sioux and Cheyenne women and children could be seen fleeing to the north and west. Turning in his saddle and waving his hat, Custer shouted, "We've caught them napping."[6] His troops cheered at the news. From the bluff, Custer could also see Major Reno beginning to attack a mile away.

Custer hurried his troopers ahead, looking for a way to cross the river and join the fight from the north. They advanced five miles downstream behind the bluffs at a fast trot, filing into a ravine and turning west for the river. He ordered trumpeter Giovanni Martini to ride back with a message. Custer's adjutant, Lieutenant W. W. Cooke, scribbled the order: "Benteen, Come on—big village—be quick—bring packs. W. W. Cooke. . . ."[7] The horsemen advanced at a rapid pace down a large ravine called South Medicine Tail Coulee. Custer intended to cross the river and thrust into the village from the west. He still confidently believed his troops could cut off the Indians who were fleeing from Reno.

Rounding a bluff, however, an unexpected sight suddenly confronted Custer. Hundreds of Sioux and Cheyenne warriors were charging on horseback across the river. With sudden fury, this great swarm of Indians came at him. Quickly, he ordered his men to dismount. He rushed them into defensive formation in two groups, one commanded by Captain Miles Keogh and the other by Captain George Yates. Indian boys and squaws shot arrows from among the trees. Hundreds of warriors on ponies circled all around.

All the while more Indians streamed across the Little Bighorn. Some attacked Yates's troops, while others moved up Medicine Tail Coulee and harassed Keogh's men, who were strongly posted on a hill. When Yates's troopers fell back, the two cavalry commands united on a height since called Battle Ridge. Custer stared in disbelief as growing numbers of Indians pressed close all around. The Indians came, stated a Sioux, "without discipline, like bees swarming out of a hive," filling the ravines and advancing up the ridge.[8] Sioux and Cheyenne on horseback circled the surrounded soldiers, shooting their rifles and sending arrows whizzing through

At the Battle of the Little Bighorn, Lieutenant Colonel George Armstrong Custer faced the greatest challenge of his military life.

the air. The hillsides became thick with dust and gun smoke. Screams and yells echoed across the battlefield. Now the Indians outnumbered the cavalrymen nearly ten to one.

On the crest of the ridge stood Custer, firing his pistol and shouting orders. Retreat was impossible. Death stared him in the face. During his career as a soldier in the Civil War and later as an Indian fighter on the western plains, Custer had faced many desperate situations. Every time, his luck and daring had seen him through. An officer who knew him once remarked, "Custer was a man of boundless confidence in himself and great faith in his lucky star. . . . He was perfectly reckless in his contempt of danger."[9]

At Little Bighorn, however, Custer's luck would run out on June 25, 1876. The battle would become known as Custer's Last Stand. George Armstrong Custer, who had thirsted for lasting fame and battlefield glory all his life, would soon meet his final fate.

2

A CADET AT WEST POINT

"George was a wide awake boy," a childhood friend remembered, "full of all kinds of pranks. . . ."[1]

George Armstrong Custer was born in New Rumley, Ohio, on December 5, 1839. In 1836, Emanuel Custer, a widower with three children, had married Maria Ward Kirkpatrick, a recent widow with two children of her own. The first two children Emanuel and Maria had together died in infancy, but their third child, George Armstrong, was strong and healthy. They called him Armstrong, but as he grew and learned to talk, he pronounced his own name "Autie," and it became his nickname. In time, three

more sons and a daughter would be born into the Custer family: Nevin in 1843, Thomas in 1845, Boston in 1848, and Margaret in 1852.

New Rumley Boyhood

Emanuel Custer worked as a blacksmith and a farmer. Autie spent many hours in the family black-smith shop, listening to his father, a loyal Democrat, discuss politics, and watching his father pound iron horseshoes into shape. While very young, Autie Custer learned to ride, sitting bareback, guiding newly shoed horses around the shop.

On the farm, young Custer fed the cows and pigs. Emanuel Custer gave each of his sons a piglet to raise. Autie planted seeds and pulled weeds in the garden. He guided the plow in the springtime and helped with the harvest in the fall. In the winter, he chopped firewood. When the local volunteer militia, the New Rumley Invincibles, marched on parade, Autie often marched beside them, dressed in a small uniform sewn by his mother, carrying a toy musket and a wooden sword.

At the age of six, Autie Custer began attending New Rumley's one-room log schoolhouse. He was smart, but he rarely did his homework. He preferred to joke and play. For a time as a teenager, Custer was apprenticed to a furniture maker in the town of Cadiz. But he failed to take an interest in that trade, so his parents sent him to a school in Monroe, Michigan.

To Monroe and Back

Monroe, Michigan, stood thirty-five miles south of Detroit on the western shore of Lake Erie. Custer's older half sister Ann lived there with her husband, David Reed. Custer spent most of the next three years with the Reeds. He attended the New Dublin School there and later the Stebbins Academy for Boys. In early 1855, he returned to New Rumley and entered the McNeely Normal School, a boarding school in Hopedale. At sixteen years of age, he impressed his fellow students. One boy remembered, "Custer was what he appeared. There was nothing hidden in his nature. He was kind and generous to his friends; bitter . . . towards his enemies."[2]

When he finished at McNeely, Custer accepted a teaching position in District Number Five in Cadiz in the summer of 1856. Many of the local girls thought he was handsome. On evenings and weekends, he attended dances, picnics, parties, and spelling bees.

The Power of a Congressman

In May 1856, Custer decided to try for an appointment to the United States Military Academy at West Point, New York. West Point provided cadets, as the students were called, with a free college education. Custer felt sure he would like military life. Every year, each United States congressman had the power to choose one young man from his district for admission. Custer wrote a hopeful letter to the

Honorable John A. Bingham, his local United States congressman. Bingham later recalled,

> I received a letter from a boy that captivated me wonderfully. . . . It was a boy's letter, in a boyish hand, but the writing . . . showed a firmness of purpose, a determination to succeed seldom apparent in one so young. And I was struck with the originality and blunt honesty of his expressions.[3]

Bingham decided to help the boy. In January 1857, Custer received his academy appointment from United States Secretary of War Jefferson Davis.

West Point

Custer entered West Point in June 1857.[4] The United States Military Academy, founded in 1802, stood on a high bluff above the Hudson River. Custer soon wrote to a friend, "I think it is the most romantic spot I ever saw."[5] Custer joined sixty-seven other new cadets arriving from all over the country. As members of the class of 1862, they

The First Women at West Point
On October 8, 1975, President Gerald Ford signed the law that allowed women to attend the United States Military Academy for the first time. Of the original 119 women who entered West Point in the class of 1980, 61 survived the difficult training and study and graduated four years later.

would attend the academy for a five-year program of study.

At sixteen, Custer stood nearly six feet tall. He was a sturdy boy with bright blue eyes and golden yellow hair. His fellow cadets thought his complexion so fair and girlish that they teasingly nicknamed him Fanny.

From June to the end of August 1857, Custer and his classmates were in summer camp, where they learned the basics of drill. In the fall, the new cadets moved into the old North Barracks, a four-story, stone dormitory building. Each room had a window, a fireplace, two beds, two chairs, a table, and other simple furnishings. Custer enjoyed chatting with his first-year roommate, James P. Parker of Missouri, and their next-door neighbor, Thomas Lafayette Rosser of Texas. Few could resist Custer's charm. One friend insisted that Custer was "the most popular man in his class."[6]

In class, the cadets studied such subjects as mathematics, English, French, Spanish, drawing, geology, chemistry, philosophy, geography, history, ethics, and grammar. Military subjects included infantry, artillery, and cavalry tactics; horsemanship; and swordsmanship.

Custer did not do well in his class work. One of his fellow cadets remembered, "He merely scraped through. . . . He was anything but a good student."[7] Fellow cadet Tully McCrea said Custer's problem was that "he is too clever for his own good. He is

always connected with all the mischief that is going on and never studies any more than he can possibly help."[8] At West Point, Custer was forever in trouble.

West Point cadets received points, or demerits, for such bad behavior as careless dress, tardiness, absence, or inattention at roll calls; for uncombed hair and unshaven faces; for unclean rooms and equipment. If a cadet received two hundred demerits in a year, he could be expelled. From September to December 1857, Custer received a total of ninety demerits for such crimes as visiting after hours, inattention, tardiness, throwing snowballs, and playing cards. By June 1858, his total of 151 demerits was the highest in his class.[9]

Custer found he could lower his number of demerits by performing extra guard duty. As a military post, West Point's gates and equipment were constantly guarded. Custer spent sixty-six Saturdays during his years at the academy doing extra

Although he managed to sit still for his graduation portrait, Custer's boisterous energy often got him into trouble during his years at West Point.

guard duty. "He had more fun," declared Cadet Peter Michie, "gave his friends more anxiety, walked more tours of extra duty, and came nearer to being dismissed more often than any other cadet I have ever known."[10]

The Problems of Slavery and States' Rights

In the fall of 1860, a crisis threatened peace in the United States. For more than forty years, the moral issue of slavery and its expansion had threatened to split the United States in two. Thousands of European immigrants provided a cheap labor force in the many factories in the North. Most Northerners had no use for slavery, and many believed it to be cruel and immoral. In the South, however, owners of cotton, rice, and tobacco plantations depended on slave labor. In the fall of 1860, Northerners elected Abraham Lincoln of Illinois the sixteenth president of the United States. Many Southerners feared that Lincoln, a member of the antislavery Republican party, would abolish slavery. They insisted that the federal government had no right to force laws upon the individual states.

After Lincoln's election, all the Southern cadets at West Point had decided to resign from the academy if their states chose to leave the United States. "You cannot imagine how sorry I will be to see this happen," Custer wrote to his sister, Ann Reed, "as

the majority of my best friends . . . have been from the South."[11]

South Carolina seceded, or withdrew, from the Union on December 20, 1860, followed over the next several weeks by Georgia, Florida, Alabama, Mississippi, Louisiana, and Texas. One by one, the cadets from these states began to leave for home. One fellow cadet predicted, "Custer, my boy, we're going to have war."[12]

In February 1861, Southern delegates met in Montgomery, Alabama, and formed the Confederate States of America. They elected Jefferson Davis as their president. On George Washington's birthday, February 22, 1861, the West Point band played the stirring notes of "The Star-Spangled Banner" on the academy parade ground. From the window of his room, Custer roared out a patriotic cheer for the Union. Southerners, led by Custer's best friend, Thomas Rosser, answered from their windows with shouts for "Dixie." "Cheer followed cheer," recalled cadet Morris Schaff, "Rosser at one window, Custer at another."[13]

The Outbreak of Civil War

On April 14, 1861, the final break between the North and South occurred when Fort Sumter, a federal fort in the harbor of Charleston, South Carolina, surrendered to Confederate forces. Within a week, another thirty-seven Southern cadets, including Tom Rosser, started for home to

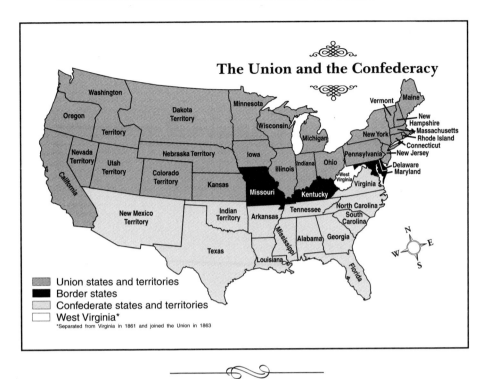

The Union and the Confederacy

Union states and territories
Border states
Confederate states and territories
West Virginia*
*Separated from Virginia in 1861 and joined the Union in 1863

The Civil War split the states in loyalty to the Union or the new Southern Confederacy. West Point cadet George Custer remained fiercely loyal to the Union.

volunteer for military service in the Confederate Army.

The senior cadets who remained at West Point prepared for active duty. It was decided that Custer's class of 1862 should be hurried ahead and graduated in June 1861. Custer and his classmates studied in a single month a course of instruction that would substitute for their entire fifth year. Toward the middle of June, Custer noted that "the class are beginning to look thin and pale," from the lack of

First in His Class

Patrick H. O'Rorke graduated first in the West Point class of June 1861. Two years later, on July 2, 1863, while colonel of the 140th New York Infantry Regiment, O'Rorke would die a hero's death, defending a hill called Little Round Top, at the Battle of Gettysburg.

sleep and amount of study.[14] The second class of 1861 graduated on June 24, with Custer ranked last.

Custer the mischief maker almost failed to graduate at all. While on guard duty in June 1861, he failed to stop a fight between two cadets. Instead, he shouted, "Stand back, boys; let's have a fair fight."[15] Custer was arrested and brought before a court-martial. The need for new officers in the army was so great, however, that the charges against him were soon dropped. On July 18, with orders to report for duty at Washington, D.C., Custer boarded a steamboat and headed south.

3

YOUNG CAVALRY OFFICER

Αt the Department of War in Washington, D.C., Custer learned he was assigned to Company G, 2nd United States Cavalry. His regiment, along with the rest of the Union Army under the field command of Brigadier General Irvin McDowell, was located at Centreville, Virginia.

The Battle of Bull Run

Through the night of July 20, 1861, Custer rode south to Virginia. When he reached army field headquarters at Centreville, he learned there would be a fight near Manassas, twenty miles away, the next morning. Custer hurried ahead to find his regiment. "So filled did I find the road with soldiers," he later

recalled, "that it was with difficulty my horse could pick his way along the sleeping bodies without disturbing them."[1] Finally Custer found his cavalry company near a creek called Bull Run. Just three days after leaving West Point, he prepared to enter battle.

The 2nd United States Cavalry Regiment had orders to protect cannons on the right flank of the Union battle line. As the fighting erupted, Confederate artillerymen sometimes fired cannonballs in Custer's direction. "I remember well," he later recalled, "the strange hissing . . . sound of the first cannon shot I heard as it whirled through the air."[2]

Through the long day of fighting, Custer watched Union infantry regiments charge in attack up Henry Hill. Late in the afternoon, a Confederate brigade just arrived on the battlefield made a surprise counterattack. "We saw the Confederate flag floating over a portion of the line just emerging from the timber," Custer exclaimed. "The next moment the entire line levelled their muskets and poured a volley into the backs of our advancing regiments on the right." Union soldiers, seized with panic, threw down their muskets. "The long lines of Union soldiery . . . ," Custer declared, "suddenly . . . became one immense mass of fleeing, frightened creatures."[3]

Custer remained calm. His company was one of the last to leave the battlefield. When a mob of frantic Union troops jammed a narrow bridge during the retreat, Custer reformed them and got them clear. Company G's bugler, Joseph Fought, exclaimed, "Custer never let up, never slackened control."[4]

Through the night, the beaten Union Army hurried through a rainstorm back to Washington and its suburbs. Custer recalled, "I scarcely waited for my company to be assigned to its camp before I was stretched at full length under a tree, where . . . I soon fell asleep, despite the rain and mud, and slept for hours without awakening."[5]

The Army of the Potomac

Stunned by the Union defeat at Bull Run, President Lincoln selected a new general to command the Union Army in Virginia. Major General George McClellan spent the summer of 1861 reorganizing the army. For several weeks, Custer served on the staff of Brigadier General Philip Kearny. In the fall, however, Custer fell ill and was granted a leave of absence. Through the winter, he stayed with the Reeds in Monroe. When he finally returned to duty, he discovered that McClellan had created the Army of the Potomac. Full of pride, the grand new army prepared for a spring campaign in Virginia.

On March 9, 1862, the Confederates abandoned their lines around Centreville and fell back toward Richmond, the Confederate capital. McClellan developed a plan to advance on Richmond from the Virginia Peninsula between the York and James rivers. The movement required shifting his entire

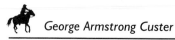
army from Washington by sea. Custer joined the 120,000 Union troops who traveled by boat to the peninsula. McClellan slowly started his army marching in April 1862 but stopped when he discovered Confederate troops entrenched at Yorktown.

Custer the Balloonist

At Yorktown, Custer was to report as an assistant to Lieutenant Nicholas Bowen, the chief engineer on General W. F. Smith's staff.[6] Traveling with the Union Army was a balloonist, Professor Thaddeus Lowe. Lowe had developed a portable hydrogen generator that could fill a silk balloon and make it rise high into the air.

Custer was ordered to scout the enemy lines by going up in Lowe's balloon. Custer carried with him field glasses and drawing materials to look at and sketch the camps of the Confederates.

A Union officer rises into the air aboard Professor Thaddeus Lowe's hot-air balloon. On the ground, soldiers hold the ropes that keep the balloon from floating away.

Clutching the sides of the little willow basket, Custer and one of Lowe's assistants rose one thousand feet into the air. "Guns could be seen mounted and . . . men . . . collected in groups, intently observing the balloon," Custer declared. "After noting such of my observations as were deemed important, I signified my desire to descend . . . and we were gradually lowered to the ground."[7]

General Smith sent Custer up, alone, three more times after that. On the night of May 3, while aloft in the balloon, Custer discovered that the Confederates had abandoned Yorktown and were retreating up the peninsula.

Gaining Attention

The Union Army pursued the Confederates as they retreated. On the morning of May 5, 1862, the Union troops caught up with them at Williamsburg, the old colonial capital of Virginia. During the fight that followed, Custer served as a volunteer aide to Brigadier General Winfield Scott Hancock. As Hancock's cheering brigade charged forward, Custer spurred his horse and led the way into the midst of the Confederates. Single-handedly, he captured six Confederate soldiers and a large silk battle flag. It was the first enemy flag ever taken by the Army of the Potomac. "[I] was in the thickest of the fight from morning till night," Custer later boasted to Ann Reed.[8]

By May 20, 1862, General McClellan's army had advanced to the Chickahominy River just a few miles from Richmond. Engineer officers examined the river for places to make a crossing. In several places, Custer bravely waded into the waters to test the depth. At any moment, hidden enemy sharpshooters might have taken a shot at him, but Custer never hesitated.

During a trial crossing on May 24, Custer, with several companies of infantry and cavalry, encountered the enemy at New Bridge. Lieutenant Bowen reported: "Lieutenant Custer . . . was the first to cross the stream, the first to open fire upon the enemy, and one of the last to leave the field."[9] When General McClellan heard of the affair, he immediately sent for Custer. McClellan asked the brave young officer if he would like to serve on his personal staff with the brevet, or temporary, rank of captain. His muddy uniform still dripping with water, Custer gratefully accepted.

Taking Time for Courtship

The Northern and Southern armies battled again at Fair Oaks, Virginia, at the end of May 1862. After that fight, General Robert E. Lee took command of the Confederate Army of Northern Virginia. Lee chose to strike McClellan in a series of bloody battles in June called the Seven Days. Stunned by these bold attacks, the Union forces fell back in retreat toward the James River. Custer's staff duty kept

Magazine artist Alfred Waud drew this sketch after witnessing Custer's crossing of the Chickahominy River in May 1862. Custer's bravery soon won him an appointment to General George McClellan's personal staff.

him on horseback delivering messages, guiding brigades, and directing the removal of the wounded. He spent four days in a row in the saddle, hardly sleeping. General McClellan later remarked, "Custer was simply a reckless, gallant boy, undeterred by fatigue, unconscious of fear."[10] That summer, Custer shot and killed his first Confederate during a skirmish near White Oak Swamp, Virginia.

Unhappy with McClellan's leadership, President Lincoln replaced him with Major General Ambrose

Burnside in November 1862. Custer very much regretted seeing McClellan depart. Temporarily relieved of duty, Captain Custer returned to Monroe, Michigan, to await new orders. At a party on Thanksgiving Day, he met twenty-year-old Elizabeth "Libbie" Bacon. Pretty, blue-eyed, brown-haired Libbie made a great impression on him. During the next weeks, Custer often strolled in front of the Bacon home, hoping for a glimpse of her. Judge Daniel Bacon disapproved of Custer's attention toward his daughter. He had noticed that Custer had celebrated his return to Monroe by getting publicly drunk. Libbie, however, was attracted by Custer's passion. "He acts it, speaks it from his eyes, and tells me every way *I love you*," she confided in her journal.[11]

Fighting Stuart's Cavalry

Custer rejoined the Army of the Potomac in the spring of 1863. Brigadier General Alfred Pleasonton, commander of the 1st Cavalry Division, had invited Custer to become part of his staff. Custer considered Pleasonton a good cavalry officer and wrote that "my position is a desirable one to a person fond of excitement."[12]

Lee's Confederate Army had won a decisive battle at Chancellorsville, Virginia, in May. Now, he boldly started his army northward. Major General J.E.B. Stuart commanded Lee's cavalry, guarding the Confederate Army's flank.

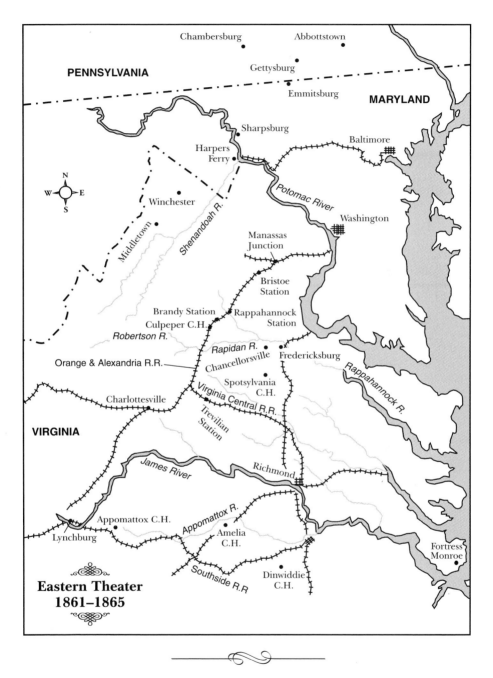

Chambersburg   Abbottstown

PENNSYLVANIA

Gettysburg

Emmitsburg

MARYLAND

Sharpsburg

Harpers
Ferry

Baltimore

Potomac River

N
W   E
S

Winchester

Washington

Middletown

Shenandoah R.

Manassas
Junction

Bristoe
Station

Brandy Station   Rappahannock
Culpeper C.H.   Station

Robertson R.

Rapidan R.

Orange & Alexandria R.R.

Chancellorsville   Fredericksburg

Rappahannock R.

Spotsylvania
C.H.

Charlottesville

Virginia Central R.R.

Trevilian
Station

VIRGINIA

James River

Richmond

Appomattox C.H.

Appomattox R.

Amelia
C.H.

Lynchburg

Southside R.R

Dinwiddie
C.H.

Fortress
Monroe

**Eastern Theater
1861–1865**

*Custer fought with the Army of the Potomac in many of the battles
in the Eastern Theater.*

The Union and Confederate cavalries finally clashed at Brandy Station, Virginia, on June 9, 1863, in the largest cavalry battle of the war. During the fight, when two Union cavalry regiments became surrounded by Confederate horsemen, Custer led several stinging counterattacks to help Union forces cut through to safety.

In a sharp skirmish at Aldie, Virginia, on June 17, 1863, Custer led another charge. Unfortunately, his skittish horse carried him far ahead of his men into the midst of the enemy. Swinging his saber left and right, Custer luckily came galloping out of the fray, breathless but unhurt. "I was surrounded by rebels and cut off from my own men, but I made my way out safely," he later boasted.[13]

Promotion

Everyone at Pleasonton's headquarters knew that Custer was ambitious. While in Michigan the previous winter, Custer had applied to Governor Austin Blair for command of the 5th Michigan Cavalry Regiment. But Blair, a Republican, had refused to consider Custer because he was only twenty-three years old and a Democrat.

On June 28, 1863, when Custer returned after a tiring day of staff duty, one of his fellow staff officers mocked, "Good evening, General." Another jokingly snapped to attention and announced, "Let me congratulate you, General." Other officers laughed loudly until Custer grew angry. "Laugh all you please," he told them. "I'll be a general yet before this is over. Wait and see."[14] When the laughter stopped, a friend took Custer's arm and led him to his tent. On the table lay a surprise, an official envelope addressed to Brigadier General George Armstrong Custer.

Major General George G. Meade, the newest commander of the Army of the Potomac, was reorganizing the cavalry. With Pleasonton's approval, Meade had promoted Custer and two other captains to the brevet rank of brigadier general. Captain, major, lieutenant colonel, colonel, brigadier general—overnight Custer had risen like a skyrocket through the ranks. At the age of twenty-three, he proudly sewed a single star on each of his shoulders to indicate his new rank. He had become the youngest general in the Union Army.

When asked which command he preferred, Custer requested the 2nd Brigade of the 3rd Cavalry Division. Called the Michigan Brigade, it drew all of its regiments (the 1st, 5th, 6th, and 7th) from the state of Michigan. Custer nicknamed the outfit the Wolverine Brigade. "The regiment of which I attempted to obtain the colonelcy (Fifth) belongs to my brigade," he gleefully explained, "so that I rather outwitted . . . Governor [Blair] who did not see fit to give it to me."[15]

4

CUSTER EARNS HIS STAR

"H"e was clad in a suit of black velvet, elaborately trimmed with gold lace, which . . . almost covered the sleeves of his cavalry jacket," remembered Michigan Captain James H. Kidd after seeing Custer for the first time. "The wide collar of a blue navy shirt was turned down over the collar of his velvet jacket, and a necktie of brilliant crimson was tied in a graceful knot at the throat."[1]

The Battle of Gettysburg

On the morning of June 29, 1863, Custer, dressed in his showy uniform, rode north from Frederick, Maryland, to Abbottstown, Pennsylvania, to take command of his brigade. The Michigan Cavalry

Custer posed for famed photographer Mathew Brady in 1864, dressed in the kind of unusual uniform he liked to wear because it attracted so much notice.

Brigade contained about twenty-five hundred troopers. Many were armed with Spencer carbines, a weapon that could fire seven shots before reloading. The brigade also included the six cannons of Battery M, 2nd United States Artillery. Soldiers of the brigade who first saw the twenty-three-year-old general joked, "Who is the child?"[2] Almost at once, the men were calling Custer "The Boy General."

The morning after Custer took command, a great battle erupted near the town of Gettysburg, Pennsylvania. On the afternoon of July 2, Custer took his brigade into action. The 6th Michigan discovered Confederate cavalry south of Hunterstown near Gettysburg. Sixty troopers of Company A soon formed in the road for an attack. It was not the duty of a brigade commander to lead a charge, but Custer rode to the front and announced, "I'll lead you this time, boys."[3]

The little company of Union troopers galloped down the road and slammed into a mass of six hundred Confederate riders, an entire Confederate brigade. Custer's horse was wounded, throwing Custer to the ground. A Confederate cavalryman aimed his carbine at the young general, within six feet of his head, but Union private Norvill Churchill shot down the man. Then Churchill pulled Custer up onto the back of his horse and carried him to safety. Only twenty-eight of the sixty troopers who made the reckless charge escaped. Custer's rashness nearly cost him his life, but his personal bravery won the respect of his men.

On July 3, 1863, the third day of the Battle of Gettysburg, six thousand Confederate cavalrymen under Major General J.E.B. Stuart clashed with five thousand Union cavalrymen near the Hanover Road, three miles east of Gettysburg. Stuart hoped to create confusion behind the Army of the Potomac, while thirteen thousand Confederate infantry charged the center of the Union defenses on Cemetery Ridge.

At 4:00 P.M., two of Stuart's cavalry brigades galloped forward to sweep the Union soldiers from the field. Only five hundred of Custer's Michigan troopers were positioned to stop more than two thousand Confederate horsemen. Spurring his horse, Custer led the charge among the enemy. Swinging his saber, he shouted, "Come on, you Wolverines!"[4] Cheering wildly, the Michiganders followed their brave brigadier, slashing, stabbing, and shooting at the Confederates. The Union troopers' furious attack stunned the Confederates and forced them to retreat. Of the Michigan Brigade, 219 men were killed, wounded, or missing during the Battle of Gettysburg, but Stuart's famed Confederate cavalry had been forced to turn back.

Following the Confederate Retreat

Robert E. Lee's entire Confederate Army had been defeated at Gettysburg. In the eleven days following

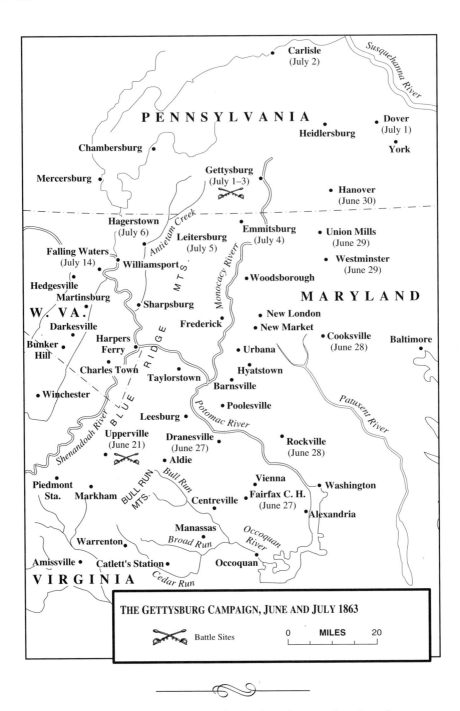

CARLISLE
(July 2)

Susquehanna River

PENNSYLVANIA

Dover
(July 1)

Heidlersburg

York

Chambersburg

Mercersburg

Gettysburg
(July 1–3)

Hanover
(June 30)

Hagerstown
(July 6)

Antietam Creek

Leitersburg
(July 5)

Emmitsburg
(July 4)

Union Mills
(June 29)

Westminster
(June 29)

Falling Waters
(July 14)

Williamsport

Monocacy River

Woodsborough

MARYLAND

Hedgesville

Martinsburg

Sharpsburg

New London

New Market

W. VA.

Darkesville

Frederick

Cooksville
(June 28)

Baltimore

Bunker
Hill

Harpers
Ferry

Urbana

Charles Town

Taylorstown

Hyatstown

Barnsville

Winchester

Shenandoah River

B L U E   R I D G E

Poolesville

Leesburg

Potomac River

Patuxent River

Upperville
(June 21)

Dranesville
(June 27)

Rockville
(June 28)

Aldie

Piedmont
Sta.

Markham

Vienna

Washington

Centreville

Fairfax C. H.
(June 27)

Alexandria

B U L L   R U N   M T S.

Bull Run

Manassas

Occoquan River

Warrenton

Broad Run

Amissville

Catlett's Station

Occoquan

VIRGINIA

Cedar Run

THE GETTYSBURG CAMPAIGN, JUNE AND JULY 1863

⚔ Battle Sites

0   MILES   20

Custer's reckless but daring leadership during the Gettysburg campaign won him the respect and admiration of his fellow soldiers.

the battle, the Union cavalry closely followed Lee's retreat back to Virginia. On July 14, at Falling Waters, Maryland, on the northern bank of the Potomac River, Custer's brigade attacked the rear guard of Lee's army.

The Union troops poured over the Confederate defenses and drove the Confederates across the river. The Michigan Brigade captured more than fifteen hundred prisoners. In that violent fight, Michigan Private Victor E. Comte saw Custer "plunge his saber into the belly of a rebel who was trying to kill him. You can guess how bravely soldiers fight for such a general."[5] In just two weeks' time, Custer had won the complete confidence of his brigade. Northern newspapers began calling Custer the "Boy General with the Golden Locks," and his troopers cheered him as "Old Curly."[6] Soon everyone in the

At Falling Waters, Maryland, on July 14, 1863, the 6th Michigan Regiment of Custer's cavalry brigade charged the rear guard of Robert E. Lee's Confederate Army and captured many prisoners.

Custer's Vow

In 1862, Custer vowed not to cut his hair until he entered Richmond. He had kept that promise, causing his West Point friend Tully McCrea to remark in the summer of 1863 that "now his hair is about a foot long and hangs over his shoulders in curls just like a girl."[7] Although he finally did cut his hair many months before Richmond was captured in 1865, Custer often liked to wear it long.

brigade had begun wearing a red necktie like the one Custer wore.

On the Banks of the Rappahannock

At the end of July 1863, Meade's Union troops followed Lee's Confederates south into Virginia as far as the Rappahannock River. Through August and September, the two enemy armies faced each other across the river. Custer busied himself during these weeks, supplying and training his men. In August, the 1st Vermont Cavalry Regiment joined Custer's brigade for a time. Like their Michigan comrades, they became fiercely loyal to their commander. Custer proudly wrote, "here, surrounded by my little band of heroes, I am loved and respected. . . ."[8]

On September 13, 1863, during a skirmish with Confederate cavalry near Culpeper, Virginia, an artillery shell exploded near Custer. A metal fragment ripped through his boot, causing a painful gash on his foot. Given twenty-seven days' furlough to nurse his injury, Custer boarded a train for Monroe. Custer used the opportunity to court Libbie Bacon. He took her walking and sat near her in church. At a party on September 28, 1863, he proposed to her and she accepted. She insisted, however, on getting her parents' consent before they married. She confided to her diary, "Yes, I love him devotedly. Every other man seems so ordinary beside my own bright particular star."[9]

Another Fight at Brandy Station

In October 1863, Custer returned to his brigade, ready for battle. Within days, on October 11, Stuart's Confederate cavalry nearly trapped one of Pleasonton's divisions at Brandy Station during an unsuccessful Union cavalry raid. At the head of the Michigan Brigade, Custer discovered a large force of Confederate cavalry in front of him led by his West Point classmate Brigadier General Thomas Rosser. Another large Confederate force led by Brigadier General Fitzhugh Lee was closing in behind. Calmly, Custer suggested that he lead a saber charge and try to cut an opening for the Union division to ride through back to the Rappahannock. Nodding his head, Pleasonton quickly agreed and ordered, "Do your best!"[10]

Custer commanded his men to draw their sabers. He said, "Boys of Michigan, there are some people between us and home; I'm going home, who else goes?" His troopers shouted hoarsely that they would. In the charge of the 1st and 5th Michigan regiments that followed, Custer would remember, "I never expect to see a prettier sight. I frequently turned in my saddle to see the glittering sabres advance in the sunlight."[11] Custer had two horses shot from under him before his Union troops finally succeeded in slicing through the Confederate line. The Union division was able to get back to safety.

The Buckland Races

Several days later, during another clash at Buckland Mills, Virginia, Custer did less well. Overwhelmed by a larger Confederate force, the Union troops fled in disorder. "Yesterday, October 19th, was the most disastrous this Division ever passed through," Custer admitted in a letter.[12] The Confederates later called the Union retreat the Buckland Races. It was a defeat in which the entire 3rd Division wagon train—including Custer's headquarters wagon and his tent, desk, and personal papers—was captured.

Through most of the winter, Meade's and Lee's armies remained encamped. The Rappahannock and the Rapidan rivers provided the barrier between the two enemy forces. Third Cavalry Division soldiers built log cabins to live in near Stevensburg, Virginia. That winter, Judge Bacon consented at last to let Custer marry his daughter. Custer had sworn off drinking forever, and he had established an honorable and impressive reputation as an officer. Custer

*Custer married Elizabeth "Libbie"
Bacon in February 1864.*

traveled to Monroe with
four officers from his
staff. On February 9,
1864, he and Libbie
Bacon exchanged wed-
ding vows at the First
Presbyterian Church.
During their honey-
moon, Custer took his
new bride to visit West
Point, New York City, and Washington, D.C. When
he returned to the army, he brought Libbie with
him. The newlyweds settled into a farmhouse near
Stevensburg for the rest of the winter.

Army life was new to Libbie Custer. She noticed
that the general's troops constantly snapped to
attention and saluted him. She thought the practice
seemed silly. "[D]o they all do that to you?" she
asked her husband. "You better believe they do," he
answered, "or discipline would remind them."[13]

Kilpatrick's Raid

Custer's division commander, Brigadier General
Judson Kilpatrick, devised a plan for a mounted raid
on Richmond. Kilpatrick proposed to liberate all
fifteen thousand Union prisoners held in Richmond

During their successful raid toward Charlottesville, Virginia, Custer's troopers watch a mill at Stannardsville burn to the ground on March 1, 1864.

Libbie Custer Meets Abraham Lincoln

George and Libbie Custer were deeply in love and stayed together whenever his military duties allowed. When the general rode off with his troops in the spring of 1864, Libbie moved to Washington, D.C., to wait for his return. One day, at a reception at the White House, she met Abraham Lincoln. The president took her hand and said, "So this is the young woman whose husband goes into a charge with a whoop and a shout. Well, I'm told he won't do so any more." Libbie politely answered that she thought her husband would continue to be as brave and reckless as ever. Without guessing what the future might hold, Lincoln jokingly responded, "Oh, then you want to be a widow, I see."[14]

and bring them back to the Army of the Potomac. Custer's part in the plan was to ride with a cavalry brigade fifty miles toward Charlottesville, Virginia, to draw attention away from Kilpatrick.

Custer's troops began their ride on February 28, 1864. The sturdy horsemen covered 150 miles in forty-eight hours. They destroyed the bridge over the Rivanna River and three large mills filled with grain and flour. They captured sixty prisoners, one flag, and five hundred horses, without having a single soldier killed or captured. Although Kilpatrick's troops failed to penetrate the Richmond defenses, General Meade considered Custer's part of the raid a success.

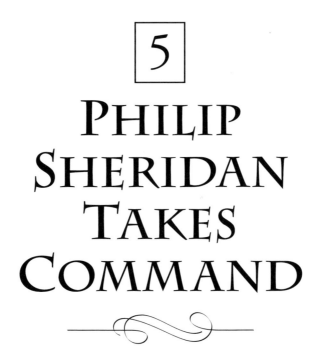

PHILIP
SHERIDAN
TAKES
COMMAND

When Lieutenant General Ulysses S. Grant took charge as general-in-chief of the Union armies in March 1864, he immediately gave command of the Cavalry Corps to thirty-three-year-old Major General Philip Sheridan. Sheridan's cavalrymen included Custer and the Michigan Brigade, which became part of the 1st Cavalry Division.

On May 3, 1864, the Army of the Potomac moved out of winter quarters and once more headed for battle. General Grant's spring campaign began two days later in the thick woods south of the Rappahannock River, called the Wilderness. During the second day of the Battle of the Wilderness, May 6, 1864, Custer's troops clashed with Confederate cavalry. These Confederate horsemen were commanded by Custer's old West Point friend Thomas Rosser.

Major Kidd remembered Custer "rode close to the very front line, fearless and resolute."[1] In the Wilderness, the Union and Confederate armies fought to a bloody draw. Instead of retreating, however, Grant shifted his army farther to the south to Spotsylvania Court House, Virginia.

Yellow Tavern

Since the start of the war, the Union cavalry in Virginia had dueled with the Confederate cavalry of J.E.B. Stuart. In all that time, the Union horsemen had never won a decisive battle. Sheridan complained that he could defeat Stuart if given the opportunity. When Grant learned of Sheridan's claim, he remarked, "Well, he generally knows what he is talking about. Let him start right out and do it."[2]

On May 9, 1864, Sheridan rode around Lee's left flank and struck south toward Richmond. His ten thousand Union cavalrymen stretched in a column thirteen miles long. To combat the threat facing the Confederate capital, on May 11, 1864, Stuart threw forty-five hundred Confederate riders across Sheridan's path at a crossroads village called Yellow Tavern, just six miles outside Richmond.

As Sheridan's three Union divisions prepared for battle, Custer spotted a weak point in Stuart's line.

Taking his own brigade and part of another, Custer charged among the Confederate cannons. One of Custer's troopers shot General Stuart through the body. Sheridan's cavalry soon overwhelmed the enemy and sent them reeling in retreat. Sheridan had whipped the Confederate cavalry just as he had predicted. Stuart's death in Richmond the next day greatly added to the South's loss.

Trevilian Station

In June, General Grant ordered Sheridan's cavalry on a raid toward Charlottesville to destroy the Virginia Central Railroad. At Trevilian Station on June 11, 1864, Major General Wade Hampton's five thousand Confederate troopers attacked Sheridan's force of six thousand men. Again Custer's brigade battled Virginian troops commanded by his old friend Thomas Rosser.

Surrounded by the enemy, Custer rallied his battered troops and

Confederate Major General J.E.B. Stuart (1833–1864). The dashing cavalry commander of Lee's army received a deadly wound during the fight at Yellow Tavern, Virginia, on May 11, 1864. Stuart's death caused mourning throughout the South.

A Twist of Fate
Private John A. Huff, Company E, 5th Michigan Cavalry, the soldier who killed J.E.B. Stuart, died within a month from a wound he received during a fight at Haw's Shop, Virginia, on May 28, 1864.

prepared them to make a desperate stand. His men dismounted and held off the Confederates with their carbines. Custer recklessly rode along the battle line, giving courage to his troops. Finally, Sheridan, with two brigades, came to Custer's rescue. The Confederates retreated, but the fight at Trevilian Station had left the Michigan Brigade with 41 men dead and 242 missing. The Confederates also captured many of the brigade's supply wagons and even seized Custer's headquarters wagon again. Custer lost all his personal belongings, his letters, field glasses, and extra uniforms. To Libbie, he wrote that they had captured "Everything except my toothbrush."[3]

Into the Shenandoah Valley

In August 1864, Sheridan received orders to advance south into the Shenandoah Valley. That part of western Virginia had been a constant problem for the Union since the start of the war. From Harpers Ferry, where the Shenandoah River joins the

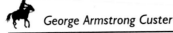

Potomac River, a wide valley of fertile farmland ran southeast behind the Blue Ridge Mountains. As they advanced, the Union troops were to burn crops, barns, and the houses of Confederate sympathizers. "In pushing up the Shenandoah Valley," Sheridan's orders read, "it is desirable that nothing should be left to invite the enemy to return."[4]

Marching with Sheridan's new forty-thousand-man Army of the Shenandoah were the 1st and 3rd Cavalry Divisions. James Taylor, an artist with *Frank Leslie's Illustrated Newspaper*, remembered seeing Custer on the march. Mounted on a black horse, Custer's "features were clear cut, his cheek-bones prominent, while his eye was steel gray with the sharpness of an eagle's glance."[5]

On September 19, 1864, Sheridan attacked Major General Jubal Early's Confederate Army of twenty thousand men at Opequon Creek near Winchester, Virginia. At an important moment in the fight, Custer sent a portion of his Wolverines charging through a brigade of sixteen hundred Confederate infantry. The charge threw the enemy into a panic. Union surgeon Harris Beecher would never forget the moment: "Oh! it was glorious to see how terror-stricken the rebels were. . . . They broke and ran in perfect dismay. The cavalry poured upon and rushed through a great herd of stampeding rebels, capturing prisoners, cannon and flags."[6]

Only nightfall saved Early's army from complete ruin. "My command . . . which entered the charge about 500 strong . . . captured over 700 prisoners," Custer gleefully exclaimed.[7]

The Burning

At the end of September 1864, Sheridan rewarded Custer with a promotion, putting him in command of the entire 3rd Cavalry Division. Though Custer was glad for the increase in responsibility, the promotion separated him from his beloved Michigan Brigade.

During the first days of October, Sheridan's army ravaged the Virginia countryside for sixty miles south of Winchester. When Lieutenant John R. Meigs of Sheridan's staff was killed by Confederate guerrillas near the village of Dayton, Virginia, Sheridan ordered Custer to burn every house in a five-mile area around the town. His troopers grimly went to work.

In the days ahead, Sheridan ordered barns, mills, haystacks, and grain fields torched throughout the valley. Valley residents would sadly remember the time as "The Burning." "When I'm finished," Sheridan boasted of the destruction, "a crow won't be able to fly through the Shenandoah without carrying his own rations."[8]

Tom's Brook

It was at Tom's Brook near Woodstock, Virginia, on October 9, 1864, that Custer once again battled his old friend Brigadier General Thomas Rosser. As their cavalry divisions prepared to fight, Custer recognized Rosser on a distant hill. Custer calmly rode out between the battle lines, sweeping his hat down to his knee in a grand salute to his old West Point comrade. Pointing to the Union general, Rosser told some of his officers, "That's General Custer, the Yanks are so proud of, and I intend to give him the best whipping to-day that he ever got."[9] But Custer had more on his mind than making a salute. He secretly scanned the enemy's line, looking for some advantage. After noting where Rosser was weakest, he rode back to his division, and the battle began.

At Tom's Brook, Virginia, on October 9, 1864, Custer saluted his old friend Thomas Rosser and also took a moment to scout enemy lines.

The 3rd Division charged across the brook, sabers waving. Rosser's Confederate line soon crumbled and began a hurried retreat. The Union troops chased the enemy a dozen miles, capturing artillery caissons, supply wagons, and ambulances. Also captured was Rosser's headquarters wagon. That night, Custer penned a teasing letter, thanking Rosser for providing him with so many nice gifts.

His victory at Tom's Brook brought Custer even greater fame. "With Custer as a leader," crowed a happy Union captain, "we are all heroes and hankering for a fight."[10] Now all of the 3rd Division troopers began wearing red ties like Custer's. They proudly called themselves "The Red Tie Boys."[11]

The Battle of Cedar Creek

Sheridan's Army of the Shenandoah settled into camp at Cedar Creek near Middletown, Virginia, in the middle of October 1864. Confederate General Jubal Early used this opportunity to make a surprise attack on the Union camp in the misty dawn of October 19. The yelling of charging Southerners shocked many drowsy Union soldiers. In the panic that followed, thousands of Sheridan's men fled from their tents. Custer's cavalry had been encamped far from the point of attack. Custer arrived near the Valley Pike to Winchester in time to see the nearby fields swarming with retreating Union soldiers.

The Confederates, however, failed to complete their morning victory. Hungry, half-naked Confederate

troops stopped to loot the hastily abandoned Union camps of food and uniforms. Custer's 3rd Cavalry Division, and those regiments of Union infantry that still remained in good order, hurriedly formed a defensive line north of Middletown. General Sheridan, who had been eleven miles away in Winchester, galloped southward as soon as he heard the roar of cannonfire. When Sheridan arrived at Cedar Creek, one of his officers suggested that the Union Army continue its retreat. Sheridan gruffly exclaimed, "Retreat—hell, we'll be back in our camps tonight!"[12] Waving his hat, the tough general rode along the battle line, shouting encouragement to the men.

That afternoon, Union troops counterattacked. Custer's two thousand cavalrymen joined the charge upon the Confederate line. The spirited attack proved too much for the tired Confederates. "Regiment after regiment, brigade after brigade, in rapid succession was crushed," recounted Confederate General John Gordon, "and, like hard clods of clay under a pelting rain, the superb commands crumbled to pieces."[13]

Frightened Confederates ran in retreat, with Custer's cavalry chasing after them. "Prisoners were taken by hundreds," exclaimed Custer, "entire companies threw down their arms, and appeared glad when summoned to surrender."[14] Custer's men captured forty-five cannons, five flags, dozens of wagons, and hundreds of prisoners. When he returned to Union Army headquarters that night, Custer was so excited he hugged Sheridan and lifted him into the air.[15]

Jubal Early's Confederate Army had been crushed at Cedar Creek. To Custer went the honor of presenting the captured flags to Secretary of War Edwin Stanton in Washington, D.C., on October 23. "General, a gallant officer always makes gallant soldiers," Stanton complimented him.[16] He also announced that Custer was being promoted to the brevet rank of major general.

6

PURSUIT TO APPOMATTOX

D on't expose yourself so much in battle," Libbie
Custer begged her husband. "Just do your
duty, and don't rush out so daringly."[1] On March 2,
1865, at Waynesboro, Virginia, Custer's division
smashed the last of the Confederate resistance in
the Shenandoah Valley. Custer's attack captured
sixteen hundred prisoners, eleven artillery pieces,
seventeen flags, and two hundred wagons and
ambulances. With the Shenandoah Valley conquered, Sheridan's cavalry swept eastward out of
the Blue Ridge Mountains. The Union horsemen cut
a path of destruction across the heart of Virginia.
They destroyed mills, warehouses, forges, and
foundries. They tore up railroad tracks and burned

Custer (seated at left) poses with his brother, Lieutenant Thomas Custer, and his wife, Elizabeth "Libbie" Custer. Throughout the war, Libbie Custer worried about her husband's safety.

bridges and station houses on the Virginia Central Railroad. "Our raid has been a chain of successes," Custer wrote to Libbie.[2]

Rejoining the Army of the Potomac

On March 27, 1865, Sheridan's cavalry reunited with the Army of the Potomac at City Point, Virginia. Within days, General Grant set in motion a plan to pry the Confederates out of their defensive trenches around Petersburg and Richmond. On March 29, Sheridan and his nine-thousand-man Cavalry Corps passed behind Lee's army and attempted to cut the Danville and Southside railroads, vital supply routes to Richmond.

The crossroads village of Five Forks, near Dinwiddie Court House, protected the Southside Railroad. On the afternoon of March 31, 1865, Confederate Major General George Pickett's nineteen thousand troops suddenly attacked Sheridan's advancing army, sending Union forces tumbling backward. Sheridan relied on Custer to prevent disaster.

A Brush With Death

In a skirmish at Ashland, Virginia, on March 15, 1865, Custer's horse tripped and turned a complete somersault, pinning Custer beneath it. If the horse had struggled to rise, its weight would have crushed Custer. But staff officers calmed the animal and gently rolled it off the general.

Heedless of danger, Custer cantered along the front, waving his hat to cheer his men. His division held up the Confederate advance and saved the Union Cavalry Corps. During the night, fifteen thousand Union infantrymen reinforced Sheridan's line. The furious battle for Five Forks continued through the next day, until the Confederate line cracked and the Southerners retreated.

The Final Chase

The Union victory at Five Forks forced General Lee to quit his weakened defenses around Petersburg and Richmond. On the night of April 2, 1865, Lee's Confederate Army fled, crossing the Appomattox River and retreating west. The next day, triumphant Union soldiers finally occupied Richmond. To pursue the retreating Southerners, General Grant turned to Sheridan's cavalry—four divisions totaling twelve thousand men. Custer's division led the chase.

During the winter, Custer's brother, Tom, had joined his staff as a lieutenant. At Namozine Church, Virginia, on April 3, Tom Custer charged his horse in among the retreating enemy and single-handedly forced three officers and eleven enlisted men to surrender with their flag. His brave act earned him the Congressional Medal of Honor.

The Confederates continued their hurried retreat westward on muddy roads. By late afternoon on April 6, Sheridan's cavalry and the Union's 6th

Infantry Corps caught up with half of Lee's army along Sayler's Creek. Custer's riders galloped furiously among the Confederates, shooting, slashing, and scattering wagons and horses. They overturned or burned three hundred vehicles.

For a second time in three days, Lieutenant Tom Custer plunged into the combat. He galloped up beside a Confederate color-bearer, grabbed the flag, and ordered the soldier to surrender. Instead, the Southerner fired his rifle in Tom Custer's face. The bullet plowed through his cheek and exited behind his ear. Tom Custer shot and killed the man, and then he galloped away, carrying the flag. For this reckless act of courage, Tom Custer would win a second Medal of Honor. Though the Confederates fought fiercely at Sayler's Creek, they were quickly overwhelmed. The Union troopers captured eight thousand men, including six generals.

To Appomattox Station

Just before sunset on April 8, 1865, Custer's cavalrymen saw ahead through the trees the depot of Appomattox Station and the smoke of locomotives. Custer waved his hat and shouted for his command to charge. The yelling Northern troopers seized three trains crammed with supplies intended for the exhausted Confederates.

Confederate cannons beyond the depot soon fired on Custer's men. Amid the glare of exploding shells, Custer led his troopers in a series of charges.

"We expected Custer would be killed every time," reported one of his cavalrymen, "but he was not scratched, [although] he had a horse or two killed under him. He really appeared to lead a charmed life."[3] By sunset, Custer's troopers had seized twenty-four cannons, two hundred wagons, and one thousand prisoners. More important, they blocked General Lee's escape route southward toward Lynchburg.

Surrender at Appomattox

Sheridan's cavalry divisions held Lee in place until the morning of April 9, 1865. When three corps of Union infantry arrived, the Confederates lost their final chance to escape. That morning, a lone Confederate officer came riding toward Custer's line, waving a white towel on a stick. The officer drew near, introduced himself as Major Robert Sims of General Longstreet's staff, and announced, "General Lee requests a suspension of hostilities."[4] As the requested truce went into effect, the gunfire along the battle line gradually stopped.

Instead of waiting to see what General Grant would do, Custer eagerly galloped toward the Confederate line, waving a white handkerchief. He demanded to see the commanding general and was brought to the headquarters of General James Longstreet, Lee's second-in-command. Assuming his angriest tone, Custer said, "In the name of General Sheridan I demand the unconditional surrender of

Major General Custer watches the approach of Confederate Major Robert Sims near Appomattox Court House, Virginia, on April 9, 1865. The Confederates asked for a truce in order to stop the fighting while General Robert E. Lee considered surrendering his exhausted army.

this army." Longstreet told the hot-headed young general, "General Lee has gone to meet General Grant and it is for them to determine the future of the armies."[5] Calming down, Custer finally returned to his division to await the outcome of that historic meeting. During the afternoon, General Robert E. Lee solemnly surrendered his Confederate Army to General Ulysses S. Grant in the home of Wilmer McLean.

After the surrender, Custer entered the Confederate camp and searched for some of his old

Sheridan's Gift

Sheridan witnessed the surrender, and afterward he paid Wilmer McLean twenty dollars for an oval pine table. Sheridan presented it to Custer as a gift for Libbie, enclosing a note,

> *My Dear Madam, I respectfully present to you the small writing table on which the conditions for the surrender of the Army of Northern Virginia were written by Lt. General Grant—and permit me to say, Madam, that there is scarcely an individual in our service who has contributed more to bring about this desirable result than your gallant husband.*

Libbie Custer treasured the gift.[6] Today it is part of the collection of the Smithsonian Institution.

West Point classmates. He desired to show them some kindness in the face of their defeat. "My husband told me," Libbie Custer later recalled, "that that night seven Confederate officers slept under the blankets in his tent."[7] In the days following the Confederate surrender at Appomattox Court House, Sheridan's cavalry rode eastward back to Petersburg. During this ride, they learned that John Wilkes Booth had assassinated President Abraham Lincoln on April 14, 1865. While Northerners mourned Lincoln's tragic death, Andrew Johnson was sworn in as the seventeenth United States president, and the last organized Confederate troops throughout the South surrendered.

The Grand Review

To celebrate the end of the war, on May 23, 1865, the Army of the Potomac marched down Washington's Pennsylvania Avenue from the Capitol to a reviewing stand erected in front of the White House. Crowds thronged the sidewalks, cheering loudly. Custer's 3rd Division rode proudly among the cavalry, each member wearing his red necktie. Custer sat on Don Juan, one of his favorite horses.

The reviewing stand erected on Washington's Pennsylvania Avenue, May 1865. President Andrew Johnson, General Ulysses S. Grant, Cabinet members, and select guests watched Custer gallop past on his excited horse, Don Juan.

As horse and rider approached the reviewing stand, someone in the crowd tossed a wreath of evergreens and flowers over the horse's neck.

"The horse became greatly excited," Dr. Pulaski F. Hyatt recalled,

> and . . . such jumps and plunges, I have never seen a horse make before, nor since. The wind had removed the General's hat, and his long, light hair was streaming in the wind. In this condition, with his horse high in air, he crossed the line in front of the President and his Cabinet. As he passed this line, his left hand firmly grasped the reins, and with the right he drew his sabre and made a salute.[8]

Many in the crowd cheered Custer's horsemanship, though some grumbled that he had spurred his horse on purpose in order to make a grand impression.

After passing in review, the 3rd Cavalry Division returned to its camp, where the men said farewell to their beloved commander. Custer and Libbie rode along the entire length of the division, receiving cheer after cheer. With the Civil War's end, the twenty-five-year-old major general now would have to adjust to another kind of military life.

7

CUSTER OF THE 7TH CAVALRY

At the end of May 1865, Libbie and George Custer enjoyed a steamboat trip down the Mississippi River. Custer had orders to join General Sheridan in New Orleans, Louisiana. Through the summer and fall, Custer, with four thousand cavalry, served on border duty along the Rio Grande and patrolled eastern Texas, enforcing federal law. With peace restored to the United States, however, by the end of the year, Custer lost his high brevet rank in the volunteer army. He was reduced to his regular United States Army rank of captain.

From General to Lieutenant Colonel

Early in 1866, Custer considered joining a foreign army. The Mexican government offered him the rank of general, with pay of ten thousand dollars yearly, in gold. When he learned that he would have to give up his United States Army commission in order to serve in Mexico, he decided against it.

By September 1866, he grabbed a new opportunity for active military duty. He accepted the rank of lieutenant colonel in the 7th Cavalry, one of four new cavalry regiments being organized in the United States Army. Within weeks, he reported for duty at Fort Riley, Kansas, located at the fork of the Republican and Smoky Hill rivers. The Custers moved into one half of a double house for officers. "Our house is so comfortable and cheery," Libbie wrote to a cousin, "for we have sunlight in the parlor all day."[1]

Colonel Andrew J. Smith was the top officer of the 7th Cavalry. But duties elsewhere prevented Smith from actively commanding the regiment. As second-in-command, Lieutenant Colonel Custer took that responsibility. Tom Custer joined the regiment as a first lieutenant, and during the early months of 1867, hundreds of new recruits also joined. Many were poor immigrants from Ireland and Germany, glad to become cavalry privates with wages of thirteen dollars a month.

The Hancock Expedition

Fort Riley was one of several posts the army had established in Kansas to protect frontier settlers from hostile American Indians. At the end of the

Great Plains Indians galloping on horseback could hunt down the buffalo upon which their lives so greatly depended.

Civil War, about two hundred seventy thousand American Indians still lived in the United States. Most of them belonged to the tribes of the Great Plains—Sioux, Cheyenne, Arapaho, Kiowa, and Comanche. Proud and independent, these American Indians roamed the land, following vast herds of buffalo. Buffalo meat, skins, and bones provided the Indians with food, clothing, shelter, and tools.[2]

In the spring of 1867, the United States government decided to relocate the Southern Cheyenne, Arapaho, and Kiowa to reservations south of the Arkansas River. The Sioux would be moved north of the Platte River. With the removal of these Indians, huge portions of Nebraska and Kansas would be available for railroad construction and homesteaders. The campaign to remove the southern tribes was assigned to Major General Winfield Scott Hancock. Hancock gathered a force of fourteen hundred troops, including the 7th Cavalry. Hancock wrote, "We wish to show [the Indians] that the government is ready and able to punish them if they are hostile."[3] In April 1867, the expedition marched to Fort Larned, where Hancock expected to meet with tribal chiefs.

On April 13, 1867, in a freezing snowstorm, Hancock's troops left Fort Larned and marched twenty-one miles upstream before camping. White Horse, a Cheyenne chief, and Pawnee Killer, a chief of the Sioux, visited the campsite, and Hancock agreed to meet with the chiefs at their village. When the troops pushed on the next morning, however, they discovered that the entire Indian village was deserted. Hancock was furious at what he believed was Indian treachery. He ordered Custer, with most of the 7th Cavalry, to chase after them.

Tracking Hostile Indians

On April 18, 1867, the 7th Cavalry reached Lookout Station beyond the Smoky Hill River. There, the troopers discovered grim evidence that the Indians were now at war against the whites. Custer wrote,

> I discovered the bodies of the three station-keepers, so mangled and burned as to be scarcely recognizable as human beings. The Indians had evidently tortured them before putting an end to their sufferings. They were scalped and horribly disfigured.[4]

Major General Winfield Scott Hancock (1824–1886) was the leader in charge of removing the southern Great Plains tribes. In 1880, Hancock became the Democratic candidate for president of the United States. He lost the election to another Civil War general, James A. Garfield.

After burying the dead men, Custer marched his command another fifteen miles to Fort Hays, having covered roughly one hundred fifty miles in four days, exhausting men and horses. Hancock, meanwhile, burned an Indian village of 251 lodges on Pawnee Fork.[5] Custer and Hancock reunited their troops at Fort Hays on May 3, 1867. Soon news began to arrive that parties of Sioux, Cheyenne, and Arapaho warriors were attacking railroad construction crews, stagecoach stations, and settlers' cabins.

Custer, with about three hundred fifty officers and men, departed Fort Hays on June 1, 1867, in search of the Indians. But it was summer now, and the prairie grass that Indian ponies fed upon was high and green. Riding strong, well-fed ponies, the Indians could easily outmarch Custer's troops. Sometimes Custer's scouts discovered Indian tracks dividing into numerous smaller parties and going off in many directions. It was nearly impossible to follow so many different trails. "I am of the opinion, . . . justified by experience, that no cavalry in the world, marching, even in the lightest manner possible . . . can overtake or outmarch the Western Indian," Custer admitted in frustration.[6]

After resting at Fort McPherson on the Platte River in Nebraska, Custer and his men pushed on to Riverside Station on the Union Pacific Railroad west of Fort Sedgwick. The final sixty miles were a hard march, and when they arrived, thirty men who had had enough of Custer and marching deserted during

Before They Became Famous

Henry M. Stanley accompanied the Hancock expedition as a reporter for the St. Louis *Democrat*. In 1871, Stanley would win worldwide fame when he found missionary David Livingstone while exploring East Africa. Also among the Hancock expedition scouts rode James Butler "Wild Bill" Hickok. "Wild Bill always carried two handsome ivory-handled revolvers of the large size," recalled Custer. During the 1870s, Hickok would become an American legend as a frontier marshal and gunfighter.[7]

the night. Although short of supplies, Custer refused to give up. He started for Fort Wallace, where there had been an Indian attack.

Before they reached Fort Wallace, the troopers discovered the bodies of Lieutenant Lyman Kidder and eleven troopers of the 2nd Cavalry Regiment. "I observed several large buzzards floating lazily in circles through the air," Custer later declared,

> [and after a search] a sight met our gaze which even at this remote day makes my very blood curdle. Lying in irregular order, and within a very limited circle, were the mangled bodies of poor Kidder and his party . . . so brutally hacked and disfigured as to be beyond recognition. . . . Every individual of the party had been scalped and his skull broken.[8]

Court-martialed

Custer and his exhausted troops finally arrived at Fort Wallace on July 13, 1867, having covered 181

Custer discovers the corpses of Lieutenant Lyman Kidder and eleven troopers during the Indian War of 1867. After killing their enemies, the Great Plains Indians often mutilated their bodies, so they would have no peace in the spirit world.

miles in a week. Custer had not seen his wife in six weeks. He had left Libbie at Fort Hays, and he suddenly feared she would try to cross Indian country to visit him or that perhaps she had fallen sick with cholera, after he heard rumors of an outbreak.

Against orders, on July 15, with an escort of four officers and seventy-two men, Custer abandoned his regiment at Fort Wallace and rushed off at a punishing pace for Fort Riley, 150 miles to the east. Without rest, Custer hurried across the Kansas plains. Horses and men, already worn out, made the march to Fort Hays in fifty-five hours. There, Custer left his escort and rode ahead by ambulance wagon with Tom Custer and a few attendants. They

arrived at Fort Riley on July 19, where he found Libbie safe and sound.

Disturbed by Custer's strange behavior, the 7th Cavalry's commanding officer, Colonel Smith, soon placed his lieutenant colonel under arrest. Among the charges made against Custer were first, "Absence without leave from his command," and second, "Conduct prejudicial to good order and military discipline."[9]

Custer sat stiffly and silently at his court-martial at Fort Leavenworth, Kansas. The trial began on September 15, 1867, and lasted almost a month. The officers who judged Custer found him guilty on all charges and sentenced him "[t]o be suspended from rank and command for one year, and forfeit his pay for the same time."[10]

Custer's first year as an army officer in the West had been a shameful failure.

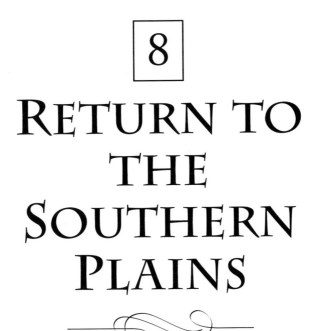

8

RETURN TO THE SOUTHERN PLAINS

an you come at once?" telegraphed General Philip Sheridan in the fall of 1868. "Eleven companies of your regiment will move about the first of October against the hostile Indians, from Medicine Lodge Creek toward the Wichita Mountains."[1]

Sheridan had persuaded the Department of War to restore Custer to duty after ten months of punishment. Sheridan had replaced Hancock as commander of the Department of the Missouri. That military department contained four military districts with six thousand troops and twenty-seven forts and camps. During the summer, Indians on the Kansas frontier had attacked homesteads on the

Saline and Solomon rivers, burning cabins, stealing livestock, and killing dozens of settlers. "I now regard the Cheyennes and Arapahoes at war," Sheridan had declared.[2]

Custer had spent most of his idle time in Monroe, Michigan. In October, he eagerly rejoined the 7th Cavalry near Fort Dodge. His return gave new life to the entire regiment. One officer recalled, "With his coming, action, purpose, energy and general strengthening of the loose joints was the order of the day."[3]

At Fort Dodge, the regiment prepared for the coming campaign. Custer trained hundreds of new recruits. To build morale, he assigned horses of a similar color to each company. One company, for example, was to ride only gray horses, another only black ones. Custer drilled his troops diligently in target practice. He put the forty best shots into a special sharpshooters' platoon. "We are going to the heart of the Indian country," Custer excitedly wrote to Libbie, "where white troops have never been before."[4]

Sheridan realized the Indians could never be caught in the warm seasons. With winter snows, however, Indian ponies grew thin and weak without sufficient grass to eat. When the snows came, the Indians encamped in villages in sheltered places. Sheridan decided to strike the Indians in the winter. According to his plan, volunteer Kansas infantry commanded by Colonel Alfred Sully and Custer's 7th Cavalry would march into the Washita River valley, where they expected to find an Indian encampment.

Camp Supply

On November 1, 1868, the Sully expedition marched south ninety miles from Fort Dodge. A huge wagon train of four hundred vehicles carried grain, rations, and clothing for the supply of the troops. Beside the Canadian River in what is now Oklahoma, Sully established a base he named Camp Supply. Soon Sheridan issued orders directing Custer and his cavalry to "proceed South . . . toward the Washita River, the supposed Winter [encampment] of the hostile tribes; to destroy their villages and ponies, to kill or hang all warriors, and bring back all women and children."[5]

Custer and his eight hundred cavalrymen prepared to march before dawn on November 23, 1868, even though a storm covered the ground with a foot of snow. At daylight, after a breakfast of corn mush and coffee, the cavalrymen, with wagons, headed south, disappearing into the swirling storm. Custer, dressed in a buffalo coat and a fur cap, led the way through the brutal blizzard. "If the storm seemed terrible to us," Custer explained, "I believed it would prove to be even more terrible to our enemies, the Indians."[6]

Three days later, while scouting, Major Joel Elliott discovered the day-old trail of perhaps one hundred fifty Indians. The cavalrymen followed the

tracks through the darkness. Their horses' hooves cracked through crusts of ice and snow until they reached the Washita River.

Discovery of a Cheyenne Village

In the early hours of November 27, 1868, Custer rode ahead with an Osage Indian scout named Little Beaver. Stopping on a bluff, they moved carefully forward on foot. In the valley below, Custer spied what appeared to be a herd of ponies. Listening carefully, he heard the bark of a dog and then the cry of an infant.

An Indian village was located on the south side of the Washita River. It contained forty-nine tepee lodges that belonged to Black Kettle's band of Cheyenne, a mixture of Indians, some peaceful and some hostile. Whispering to his officers, Custer soon divided his command into four sections, with orders to surround the village and attack at dawn.

"General," Captain William Thompson remarked, "suppose we find more Indians there than we can handle?"

Custer responded curtly, "There are not Indians enough in the country to whip the Seventh Cavalry."[7]

The Battle of Washita

Before dawn, Custer's troopers were in position. "We had approached near enough to the village now," Custer remembered, "to plainly catch a view here and there of the tall white lodges as they stood in irregular order among the trees. . . . I was about to turn in my saddle and direct the signal for attack . . . when a single rifle shot rang sharp and clear on the far side of the village."[8] Buglers immediately sounded "Charge," and the regimental band struck up "Garry Owen," an Irish tune. The musicians managed to toot only a few notes, however, before the icy air froze their instruments.

The cavalrymen dashed into the village from all directions. "The Indians," said Custer, ". . . quickly overcame their first surprise and in an instant seized their rifles, bows, and arrows, and sprang behind the nearest trees, while some leaped into the stream, nearly waist deep."[9] The Cheyenne warriors defended their village with desperate courage, while women and children huddled in the tepees or ran, screaming, across the snow-covered ground.

Custer galloped ahead, shooting down one warrior and knocking down another with his horse. The Cheyenne resisted fiercely. Captain Louis Hamilton tumbled from his saddle, shot to death. Another bullet ripped into the body of Captain Albert Barnitz, wounding him severely. "On all sides," Custer later declared, "could be heard the sharp crack of the Indian rifles and the heavy responses from the carbines of the troopers."[10]

"Our chief, Black Kettle, and other Cheyennes, many of them women and children, were killed that day," remembered a Cheyenne woman named

Kate Bighead.[11] In just ten minutes, the cavalry had captured the village. Troopers began herding together Indian women and children.

In the midst of the fight, Major Elliott had spied a group of Indians escaping on foot down the valley. Excitedly, he called for volunteers to chase after them, and soon he galloped downstream with nineteen troopers. Lieutenant Edward Godfrey, also riding downstream in pursuit of the Indians and their ponies, made a stunning discovery: "I was amazed to find that as far as I could see down the well wooded, tortuous valley there were tepees— tepees . . . [and] mounted warriors scurrying in our direction."[12] As it turned out, the Washita River valley contained many winter villages of Arapaho, Cheyenne, Kiowa, Comanche, and Apache Indians. Godfrey hurried back to report this news to Custer. Before long, Indian warriors covered the hills overlooking the defeated Cheyenne village. "We now found ourselves surrounded," recalled Custer, "and occupying the position of defenders of the village."[13]

The situation was growing more dangerous. Major Elliott and his nineteen volunteers remained missing, and all the while the Indians and the United States soldiers exchanged gunfire. Custer ordered Godfrey to take a squadron of troopers and destroy all Indian property. "I began the destruction at the upper end of the village," remembered Godfrey, tearing down tepees and piling several together on the tepee poles, set fire to them. (All tepees were made of tanned buffalo hides.) As the fires made headway, all articles of personal property—buffalo robes, blankets, food, rifles, pistols, bows and arrows . . . etc.—were thrown in the fires and destroyed.[14]

In addition, Custer ordered his men to slaughter 875 captured Indian ponies to keep them out of the hands of the Indians.

At nightfall, the cavalry regiment marched out of the Washita River valley. The surrounding Indians chose to stay and protect their villages rather than follow after them. In triumph, Custer sent a note by messenger ahead to Sheridan at Camp Supply detailing his victory. On December 2, the 7th Cavalry paraded into Camp Supply, where General Sheridan received them in review. Custer reported one officer killed, Louis Hamilton; fourteen officers and men wounded; and Elliott and nineteen troopers missing in the fight at Washita. He also stated that 103 Indians had been killed and 53 captured.

Custer, the man the Southern Cheyenne called *Hi-es-tzie*, meaning "Long Hair," soon received national fame as a successful Indian fighter.[15] Many Americans called the battle a massacre, but Philip Sheridan declared that at Washita, "the victory was complete, and the punishment just."[16]

Returning to the Battlefield

On December 7, 1868, the 7th Cavalry and Sully's Kansas volunteers rode again from Camp Supply.

*At the Battle of Washita, Custer ordered that 875 captured Indian
ponies be slaughtered.*

They headed south, back to the Washita River valley. Custer gave General Sheridan a personal tour of the battlefield. It was then that the mystery of Major Elliott's disappearance was solved.

Custer described, "we suddenly came upon the stark, stiff, naked, and horribly mutilated bodies of our dead comrades. No words were needed to tell how desperate had been the struggle before they were finally overpowered."[17]

It was clear that Elliott and his men had encountered a mass of Indians on horseback. The outnumbered troopers had defended themselves as long as they could, but they were finally overwhelmed and killed.

Taming the Southern Plains

The defeat at Washita and harsh winter weather broke the spirits of many Indians on the Southern Plains. In January 1869, Custer, with just forty-three troopers, found a camp of Arapaho and succeeded in convincing Chief Little Raven to surrender his people at Fort Sill.

In March, the 7th Cavalry, joined by volunteers of the 19th Kansas Cavalry, some fifteen hundred men in all, marched again, in search of the Cheyenne. They soon located two villages of 260 tepees on Sweetwater Creek in the Texas panhandle. Escorted into the tepee of Chief Medicine Arrow, Custer smoked a large ceremonial clay pipe and talked of peace. Custer knew these Cheyenne held two young white women as captives. He negotiated for three days about the release of captives and the surrender of the villages. In the end, he took three chiefs as prisoners and threatened to hang them unless the white women were freed. Finally, the Cheyenne freed Mrs. Anna Morgan and twelve-year-old Sarah Catherine White. The chiefs promised to report to Camp Supply as soon as their ponies could make the journey, which they did on the evening of March 28, 1869.

In three weeks, Custer had marched hundreds of miles through the wilderness. He had found and subdued the hostile Cheyenne, and he also had rescued two captive women. In a letter to Libbie, he proudly exclaimed, "I have been successful in my campaign against the Cheyennes."[18]

9

ON THE NORTHERN PLAINS

"We remained in Kansas five years," Libbie Custer would remember, "during which time I was the only officer's wife who always followed the regiment."[1] Through the spring and summer of 1869, Custer and his wife lived at Fort Hays, while companies of the 7th Cavalry served at various posts along the Kansas Pacific Railroad and patrolled the prairie. In October, the Custers and the 7th Cavalry rode to Fort Leavenworth for winter quarters.

Times of Peace

Custer spent most of 1871 on furlough from the army. He and Libbie visited Monroe, Michigan, and New York City. In New York, Custer tried to take

advantage of his fame by selling stock in a Colorado silver mine. But the mine failed to show much profit.

In September 1871, Custer and the 7th Cavalry were transferred to the South for duty. Custer and his wife lived for a time in Elizabethtown, Kentucky. While there, Custer penned a series of articles for *Galaxy* magazine. He proved to be a skillful writer. In 1874, Sheldon & Company, owners of *Galaxy*, published the articles in a book entitled *My Life on the Plains*.

A New Assignment

Custer was delighted in February 1873 to receive orders for the 7th Cavalry to report to the Dakota Territory on the Northern Plains. The Department of War had promised military protection for

Buffalo Hunter
Custer enjoyed taking part in buffalo hunts. In the summer and fall of 1869, he escorted several wealthy Englishmen, showman P. T. Barnum, and a group of Michigan friends, including Detroit Mayor K. C. Barker, on separate buffalo hunts. In January 1872, he helped host another buffalo hunt, this one arranged by the government for Russian Grand Duke Alexis Romanov. With famous guide Buffalo Bill Cody and a hundred reservation Sioux warriors, the party hunted buffalo in Kansas and Colorado.[2]

Northern Pacific Railroad surveyors going into the Yellowstone region of Montana and Wyoming.

At Camp Sturgis near Yankton in the Dakota Territory, Custer drilled his regiment and prepared it for active duty. Second Lieutenant Charles Larned complained in a letter of April 19, "Custer is not making himself at all agreeable to the officers of his command. He . . . spends his time in giving annoying . . . and useless orders which visit us like the swarm of evils from Pandora's box."[3] Custer expected much of his regiment and could sometimes be demanding, unreasonable, and unfair.

When Custer judged his troops ready, the regiment marched to Fort Rice, four hundred miles up the Missouri River, arriving in June. "It was wonderful . . . ," one enthusiastic trooper declared, "to be riding into Indian country as part of the finest regiment of cavalry in the world. We were all mighty proud of the Seventh. It just didn't seem like anything could ever happen to it."[4]

The Indians of the Northern Plains

They called themselves the Lakota, meaning "the People" in their language. But the white men labeled them with the Indian word *Sioux*, meaning "enemies" or "serpents."[5] For more than a century, the Sioux had roamed the Northern Plains, following herds of buffalo. Tough fighters, the Sioux had won control of much of the Dakota Territory and eastern Montana from the Arikara, Cheyenne, and Crow

Indians. The Sioux had numbered perhaps thirty thousand when white settlers first entered the region in the 1860s. The Sioux called the strangers *wasichus*, meaning "you can't get rid of them."[6]

A treaty signed by some Sioux chiefs at Fort Laramie in 1868 permitted the construction of railroads through the Sioux territory. But the proposed route of the Northern Pacific Railroad sliced through the heart of the Sioux's traditional buffalo range along the Yellowstone River. The United States government expected hostile bands of Sioux to resist the building of the railroad.

At Fort Rice, 79 officers and 1,451 men commanded by Colonel David S. Stanley gathered, including railroad engineers and teamsters. Hired as scouts were twenty-seven Arikara, blood enemies of the Sioux. On June 20, 1873, Stanley's Yellowstone expedition set off. Nearly three hundred wagons rattled ahead, carrying equipment and supplies. Cowboys drove along 450 head of cattle to provide the soldiers with fresh meat.

Restless and energetic, Custer rode on Dandy, his favorite horse, at the head of his regiment. Almost every day while on the march, Custer roamed miles ahead, either scouting or hunting for game. "It seemed that the man was so full of nervous energy," remarked a private, "that it was impossible for him to move along patiently."[7] On July 14, the expedition reached the Yellowstone River, and the following day, the steamboat *Far West* arrived with additional supplies. The troops pitched their tents and rested for a week.

Early on the expedition, Custer renewed an old friendship. Thomas Rosser was employed as chief engineer by the Northern Pacific Railroad and headed the survey party. The two former Civil War enemies spent many evenings together. "Well, I have joined the engineers," Custer cheerfully wrote to Libbie after his first meeting with Rosser.

> I was lying half asleep when I heard "Orderly, which is General Custer's tent?" I sprang up. "I know that voice, even if I haven't heard it for years." It was my old friend General Rosser. Stretched on a buffalo robe . . . in the moonlight, we listened to one another's accounts of the battles in which we had been opposed. It seemed like the time when, as cadets, we lay, huddled under one blanket, indulging in dreams of the future.[8]

Attacked by Indians

Toward the end of July 1873, the expedition crossed the Yellowstone River and continued marching southwest. On August 4, along the Tongue River, Custer, with ninety troopers, scouted ahead and discovered an Indian trail. Late in the morning, the soldiers stopped to rest in a grove of cottonwood trees. The shout of "Indians! Indians!" soon awakened Custer from his nap. A handful of Sioux were trying to scatter the cavalry horses. Custer, with twenty men, mounted and chased after the few Indians. Custer had ridden far ahead of his men

Confederate Major General Thomas Lafayette Rosser (1836–1910). Custer's West Point friend and Civil War enemy would loyally serve the United States in 1898 as a brigadier general during the Spanish-American War.

when suddenly, from a hiding place among the trees, nearly three hundred mounted Sioux warriors charged, their war whoops echoing across the valley.

"Wheeling my horse suddenly around," Custer later exclaimed, "and driving the spurs into his sides, I rode as only a man rides whose life is the prize."[9] He took refuge with his ninety troopers, who found themselves surrounded by the Sioux war party. The Sioux repeatedly attacked. For three hours, the troopers clung to the riverbank, sweltering in the summer heat, shooting into the high grass at the Indians who yelled and fired back. Custer's orderly dropped dead beside him, shot through the head. With their ammunition nearly finished, Custer and his men finally mounted and counter-attacked. The bold charge surprised the Sioux, who ran to their ponies and retreated. Custer had narrowly survived his first encounter with Sioux war chief Crazy Horse.

Further Adventures

The Sioux attacked the 7th Cavalry again on August 11. The troopers scrambled into a line along the Yellowstone riverbank. Hundreds of Sioux swam their ponies across the swirling river and charged Custer's position from both flanks. Custer shifted companies to meet these threats, riding along the length of the battle line. Bullets and arrows ripped through the air, but as a newspaper reporter later declared, Custer "seemed to lead a charmed life. . . . He exposed himself freely and recklessly."[10] Charging in a counterattack, Custer tumbled to the ground when his horse was killed under him. But the Indians scattered, fleeing across the river. The fight resulted in one cavalryman dead and three wounded. Custer believed his men had killed forty Sioux warriors.

The expedition marched west until August 15, when the railroad men finished their survey. After a day's rest, the column began the journey back to Dakota Territory. Custer arrived at Fort Abraham Lincoln, south of Bismark, on September 21. The Stanley expedition had covered 935 miles in 95 days. To Custer, it was all a glorious adventure.

Custer spent the winter months as commander at Fort Abraham Lincoln, enjoying dances, card parties, and sleigh rides with Libbie. He kept a pack of forty hunting dogs and, as an amateur taxidermist, stuffed foxes and birds he had shot while hunting.

The Black Hills

For over half a century, white men had whispered about gold in the Black Hills of the Dakota Territory. To the Sioux, however, *Paha Sapa*, "Hills That Are Black," was a religious place where sacred spirits dwelled.[11] Under the terms of the Fort Laramie Treaty of 1868, the Black Hills remained part of Sioux territory. Whites were forbidden to enter the forty-five hundred square miles that were included in the region.

General Sheridan had no respect for the treaty. On May 1, 1874, he won approval to establish a military post in the Black Hills. Custer would command an expedition to determine possible locations for the military post and investigate the rumors of gold. Custer declared, "The Indians have long opposed all efforts of white men to enter the Black Hills [but] I will have a well equipped force, strong enough to take care of itself . . . ten full companies of the best cavalry in Uncle Sam's service."[12]

At Fort Abraham Lincoln, Custer gathered a force consisting of the 7th Cavalry Regiment, two infantry companies, three Gatling guns, a cannon, and seventy-five Indian scouts, mostly Arikara. Civilian engineers, geologists, newspaper reporters, and teamsters brought the total to 951 people. Twenty-four-year-old Boston Custer arrived from the East to join brothers George and Tom in this new adventure.

Custer (second from left) proudly poses with a grizzly bear he shot during the Black Hills expedition. Sitting at Custer's right is his favorite Arikara scout, Bloody Knife.

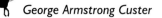

On July 2, 1874, the expedition set out. The column marched at an easy pace through lush valleys covered with wildflowers and past gurgling mountain streams into the heart of the Black Hills. Enlisted men relaxed and played baseball in the evenings. Officers enjoyed fishing and hunting. Custer climbed the hills and explored rocky caves.

On July 30, two prospectors with the expedition, William McKay and Horatio Nelson Ross, discovered flecks of gold near French Creek. Immediately, Custer sent a messenger galloping back to Fort Laramie with the exciting news. "The miners report that they found gold among the roots of the grass," Custer claimed.[13]

After exploring the region, Custer led the command into Fort Abraham Lincoln on August 30. The expedition had covered nearly nine hundred miles in sixty days. By then, the news of gold had raced across the country. By the spring of 1875, as many as fifteen thousand miners had rushed into the Black Hills. As the region swarmed with gold prospectors, the Sioux bitterly realized their treaty had been broken.

10

CUSTER'S LAST STAND

I appeal to you as a soldier," Custer wrote to President Ulysses S. Grant in May 1876, "to spare me the humiliation of seeing my regiment march to meet the enemy and I not share its dangers."[1] In March of that year, Custer had appeared in Washington, D.C., before a congressional committee. The committee was investigating corruption at military trading posts. During his testimony, Custer had hinted that President Grant's brother Orvil was involved in taking bribes in the sale of post traderships. Furious at such rumors, Grant refused to give Custer permission to return to his troops at Fort Abraham Lincoln.

There was to be another campaign against the hostile Sioux and Cheyenne that summer. During the winter, the government had announced that all Sioux and Northern Cheyenne found off their reservations after January 31, 1876, would be regarded as hostile. Now the army prepared at Fort Abraham Lincoln to march against these Indians. Only after Generals Philip Sheridan and Alfred Terry petitioned that Custer be allowed to join the expedition did President Grant finally agree. Newspaper reporter Mark Kellogg of the New York *Herald* saw Custer at Fort Abraham Lincoln in May and wrote that "Custer, dressed in a dashing suit of buckskin, is prominent everywhere. Here, there, flitting to and fro, in his quick eager way. . . . The General is full of perfect readiness for a fray."[2]

The plan of attack called for three separate army columns to meet in the Yellowstone region. Brigadier General George Crook would march north from Wyoming with nearly twenty-five hundred troops. General Terry and Lieutenant Colonel Custer would march from the east with another twenty-five hundred men. Colonel John Gibbon would join them from the west with some four hundred frontier troops. Together they hoped to find and catch the hostile Sioux and Cheyenne.

General Terry's Dakota Column consisted of the entire 7th Cavalry, three companies of infantry, and three rapid-fire Gatling guns. Arikara and Crow Indians would serve as scouts, and teamsters would drive the supply wagons. Five members of the Custer family rode with the 7th Cavalry. Lieutenant Colonel George Armstrong Custer commanded. His brother Tom was captain of C Company. His brother-in-law James Calhoun served as first lieutenant in command of L Company. His brother Boston and his nephew Harry Armstrong Reed both rode along in search of summer adventure.

Custer, dressed in a buckskin jacket, with his hair cut short for comfort in the summer heat, led the 7th Cavalry out of Fort Abraham Lincoln on May 17, 1876. It took a month for Terry's column to reach the Yellowstone River, deep in Indian land. On June 21, Terry, Custer, and Gibbon met to discuss their final plans. They guessed that the Indians were encamped either on the upper Rosebud River or in the valleys of the Bighorn or Little Bighorn rivers. It was decided that Custer and the 7th Cavalry should advance up the Rosebud and then turn toward the Little Bighorn. Gibbon and Terry would follow by different routes. Reuniting near the Little Bighorn on June 26, together they would be able to defeat any Indians they discovered. Before setting out, Custer wrote his wife, "I feel hopeful of accomplishing great results."[3]

A Battle on the Rosebud

Bands of Sioux and their Cheyenne allies had been in the Yellowstone region for months. Sitting Bull, Crazy Horse, and other Sioux leaders had long

resisted living on reservations. In early June, Sitting Bull had performed a ritual Sun Dance. After cutting fifty pieces of flesh from each of his arms, he fell into a trance and had a vision. Afterward, another warrior, Black Moon, explained to the assembled Sioux,

> Sitting Bull . . . heard a voice from above saying, "I give you these because they have no ears." He looked up and saw soldiers . . . on horseback coming down like grasshoppers, with their heads down and their hats falling off. They were falling right into our camp.[4]

The Sioux believed Sitting Bull's vision meant that soldiers who would not listen to calls for peace were coming to their camp and would be killed there.

On June 17, 1876, warriors led by Crazy Horse attacked General Crook's approaching column near the headwaters of the Rosebud River. The attack stunned Crook's men, who retreated south the next day. As Crook withdrew, the Indians moved their village to the east bank

Called Tatanka Yotanka in his native Lakota language, Sioux leader Sitting Bull's refusal to live on a reservation helped spark the Indian War of 1876.

of the Little Bighorn River. Throughout the previous weeks, reservation Sioux and Cheyenne had joined the village, swelling it to one thousand tepees, with perhaps seven thousand people, of whom two thousand were warriors.

Custer Marches Ahead

At noon on June 22, 1876, Custer and his 7th Cavalry horsemen passed in review before Terry, Gibbon, and staff officers. Lieutenant Winfield Scott Edgerly remembered the troops being eager to begin their mission against the Indians.[5] The regiment numbered 31 officers; 566 enlisted men; 35 Arikara and Crow Indian scouts; about a dozen packers, guides, and other civilians; and a train of 175 pack mules carrying supplies. Each soldier carried a Springfield single-shot carbine and a Colt six-shooter.

Fatal Mistakes

Major James Brisbin of the 2nd United States Cavalry asked that his four companies of troopers be permitted to go with Custer, but General Terry refused. Terry explained, "[Custer] is smarting under a rebuke of the President . . . and I wish to give him a chance to do something."[6] Custer also refused to take along the Gatling guns because he believed the heavy weapons would slow him on his march.

The 7th Cavalry marched up the east bank of the Rosebud River, twelve miles the first day, thirty each of the next two. On the afternoon of June 24, Custer's scouts discovered fresh Indian tracks. With feverish impatience, Custer pushed ahead. He advanced another fifteen miles during the night and into the morning of June 25.

Lieutenant Charles Varnum, chief of scouts, soon reported that the Indian village and its pony herd had been discovered. Custer quickly rode forward to see for himself. At a crest in the Wolf Mountains, later named the Crow's Nest, Custer's scouts pointed to a spot some fifteen miles in the hazy distance. Gazing through field glasses, Custer finally grumbled, "Well I've got about as good eyes as anybody and I can't see any village, Indians or anything else." Scout Mitch Bouyer promised, "General, I have been with these Indians for thirty years, and this is the largest village I have ever heard of."[7]

The great size of the village struck fear in the hearts of many of the Arikara and Crow scouts. They felt they would all die if Custer attacked. Half Yellow Face, a Crow, said to Custer, "You and I are both going home today by a road we do not know." The Arikara scout, Bloody Knife, signed to the sun with his hands and predicted, "I shall not see you go down behind the hills tonight."[8]

Custer scoffed at their fears. He hurried the 7th Cavalry forward another ten miles. Along the way, scouts saw several Sioux riding ahead and felt certain that the enemy knew of their presence. Custer believed he had to attack immediately, before the Sioux could scatter.

As the 7th Cavalry entered the Little Bighorn Valley, Custer split the regiment into four sections. Major Marcus Reno commanded 140 officers and enlisted men, Captain Frederick Benteen another 125 men. A total of about 225 men remained under Custer's immediate command. Captain Thomas M. McDougall and the eighty men of Company B would stay with the pack train.

At 12:15 P.M., Benteen set off, veering to the south in order to scout for the enemy. Soon afterward, Lieutenant W. W. Cooke delivered Custer's orders to Major Reno: "The Indians are about two miles and a half ahead, and on the jump. Follow them as fast as you can and charge them (wherever you find them) and we will support you."[9]

Reno's Attack

Reno's 140 troopers rode down into the valley, forded the river, and galloped toward the southern end of the Indian village. Their approach finally alerted the Indians. "All through that great camp was the confusion of complete surprise," declared White Bull, nephew of Sioux chief Sitting Bull.[10] "In all of the camps, as I went through them," remembered Cheyenne woman Kate Bighead, "there was great excitement. Old men were helping the young warriors in dressing and painting themselves for battle.

Some women were bringing war horses from the herds. Other women were working fast at taking down their tepees."[11]

Hurriedly mounting their ponies, hundreds of Sioux warriors advanced to meet Reno's charge. "The very earth seemed to grow Indians," Reno later reported. "They were running toward me in swarms and from all directions. I saw I must defend myself and give up the attack mounted."[12] Reno ordered his men to halt and dismount.

Many of Reno's men formed a skirmish line, while others dashed to the rear, leading the horses. The fighting was furious. Reno's skirmish line lasted hardly fifteen minutes before Sioux horsemen spilled around its left flank and got behind it. Reno ordered a withdrawal into a thick grove of trees and underbrush.

Led by Sioux chiefs Gall and One Bull, the Indians rushed at Reno's troops in growing numbers. A bullet smashed into scout Bloody Knife's head and splattered gore all over Major Reno's face and uniform. In sudden panic, Reno shouted to the men to mount and follow him. The fearful major fled the shelter of the woods. He and his troopers raced their horses to the river.

"We rode right into them, chasing them into the river," remembered Sioux warrior One Bull. "We killed many on the river bank and in the water. I rode up behind one soldier and knocked him over with my war club. Then I slid off my pony and held the soldier's head under water until he was dead."[13]

The Little Bighorn River (called the Greasy Grass by the Indians) was about forty yards wide and two to five feet deep. Reno's troopers splashed across the water as Indians crowded the banks and fired into the tangle of struggling horses and riders. The bloodied troopers took refuge on a bluff above the river. Of Reno's 140 men, 40 had been killed and 13 wounded, and more than a dozen were missing, left in the timber below.

At about 4:30 P.M., Captain Benteen's column of 125 men arrived and joined Reno's embattled troops. Benteen had received an order from Custer to come quickly. Benteen's soldiers found complete chaos on the crest of "Reno Hill." Many of Reno's men seemed gripped with terror. Reno could not give Benteen any information at all about Custer's location.

Captain Thomas B. Weir tried to lead his company to the north to rejoin Custer. Halting at a rise,

Counting Coup

The Sioux and other Great Plains Indians believed the striking of a blow or "coup" (pronounced coo) upon an enemy's person was the most glorious deed a warrior could perform. To strike first was the greatest honor. It won the warrior the right to add an eagle's tail feather to his war bonnet. The counting of coup required more bravery than shooting or scalping an enemy.

Weir's troopers saw clouds of dust in the distance and heard the sound of gunfire. Reno and Benteen followed eventually with the other companies, but increasing numbers of Sioux and Cheyenne warriors forced a withdrawal back to Reno Hill. Benteen did not join Custer as ordered but instead remained with Reno.

Battle Ridge

After leaving Reno, Custer and his 225 men had continued northwest, riding along the bluffs on the east side of the river. Custer searched for a way down to the river in order to cross and attack the Indian village from the rear. At one halt he galloped to a high bluff and saw for the first time the huge size of the village. Indian tepees filled the landscape for three miles beside the riverbank.

Sioux and Cheyenne women and children could be seen fleeing from the village. Custer's horsemen hurried on another mile down a large ravine called South Medicine Tail Coulee. Rounding a bluff, Custer suddenly saw hundreds of mounted warriors swarming across the stream toward him. There were more Indians than he had ever expected. Quickly, he dismounted his men, each fourth man holding, cavalry fashion, the horses of the other three. He sent Captain George Yates and two companies down the ravine toward the river while he remained behind with three companies commanded by Captain Miles Keogh. Warriors led by Sioux chief Gall, just arrived

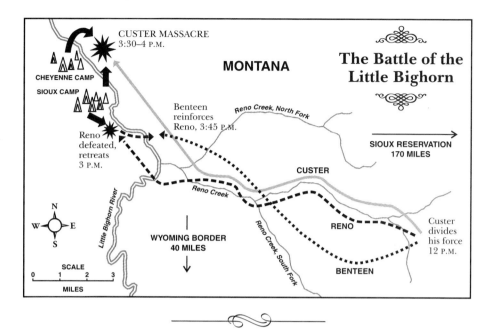

The Battle of the Little Bighorn, fought on June 25, 1876, was a military disaster, partly because each of the commanders—Custer, Reno, and Benteen—had little or no idea what the troops of the other commanders were doing.

from the Reno fight, continued to splash across the river. In the face of such large numbers, Yates's companies soon fell back and rejoined Custer and Keogh on a rise since called Battle Ridge.

More Indians poured across the Little Bighorn, led by Sioux chief Crazy Horse. They rode up and encircled the ridge from the north. Crazy Horse encouraged his men: "Ho-ka hey! It is a good day to fight! It is a good day to die! Strong hearts, brave hearts, to the front! Weak hearts and cowards to the rear!"[14]

Custer did not know that Major Reno's attack had failed or that Captain Benteen would not be coming to his aid. Now his two hundred twenty-five men faced nearly two thousand Sioux and Cheyenne warriors. Gall and his warriors opened fire on the cavalrymen holding the horses. They excited the horses by yelling and waving blankets. Dozens of horses broke loose and stampeded toward the river. "The horses . . . were running in all directions," remembered Sioux warrior White Bull. "Lots of Indians stopped shooting to capture these horses. . . . Now that the soldiers were all dismounted their firing was very fierce."[15]

Completely surrounded, without their horses, Custer's men saw that retreat was impossible. Many troopers panicked and began shooting wildly into the air. Indians with clubs and hatchets galloped close and counted coup, striking soldiers on the head and shoulders.

The hillsides became thick with dust and gun smoke. The noise of rifles, screaming, and shouting echoed across the battlefield. Gall's warriors rushed upon Battle Ridge from the south and east. Warriors led by Crow King, Crazy Horse, White Bull, Two Moon, and others attacked from the north and west. Creeping ever closer on foot, the warriors killed cavalrymen with arrows and rifle fire. "The Indians kept coming like an increasing flood which could not be checked," exclaimed Red Hawk, a Sioux.[16]

"This new battle was a turmoil of dust and warriors and soldiers," declared a Sioux warrior named Beard,

with bullets whining and arrows hissing all around. Sometimes a bugle would sound and the shooting would get louder. Some of the soldiers were firing pistols at close range. Our knives and war clubs flashed in the sun. I could hear bullets whiz past my ears.[17]

By now, the troops were spread out all along Battle Ridge. "At the end it was quite a mess," exclaimed a Sioux named Stands in Timber. "They could not tell which was this man or that man, they were so mixed up. Horses were running over the soldiers and over each other. The fighting was really close, and they were shooting almost any way without taking aim."[18] Some of the cavalrymen gathered in clusters and died together. In one group lay Miles Keogh, a trumpeter, and three sergeants. About forty men of Company E rushed off the ridge toward the river, but "We were right on top of the soldiers," a warrior stated, "and there was no use in their hiding from us."[19]

On Battle Ridge, soldiers ducked behind dead horses and kept firing their guns. They made a brave stand, but caught within a ring of arrows and bullets, the cavalrymen fell. The Sioux and Cheyenne edged nearer through the buffalo grass, dashing forward to count coup, and killing at close range.

On the crest of the ridge stood Custer. "I charged in," White Bull later claimed:

A tall, well-built soldier with yellow hair and mustache saw me coming. . . . We grabbed each other and wrestled there in the dust and smoke. . . . This soldier was very strong and brave. . . . He hit me with his fists on the jaw and shoulders, then grabbed my long braids with both hands, pulled my face close and tried to bite my nose off. I yelled for help: "Hey, hey, come over and help me!" I thought that soldier would kill me. . . . [W]e were whirling around, back and forth. . . . Finally I broke free. He drew his pistol. I wrenched it out of his hand and struck him with it three or four times on the head, knocked him over, shot him in the head, and fired at his heart.[20]

In less than one hour, Custer and every trooper with him lay dead on the grassy slopes of Battle Ridge. The Sioux White Bull described: "We had killed many soldiers. They had attacked us and meant to wipe us out. We were fighting for our lives and homeland. Cries of victory went up."[21]

"Some of the women, mourning for their own dead, beat and cut the dead bodies of the white men," explained Cheyenne woman Kate Bighead.[22] "[An] older woman poked her bone sewing awl deep into each of the white man's ears," remembered White Cow Bull. "I heard her say, 'So Long Hair will hear better in the Spirit Land.'"[23]

Aftermath of the Battle

With the defeat of Custer's companies, the warriors swarmed back to the bluff where Reno, Benteen, and the pack train remained trapped. Until the afternoon of June 26, the warriors attacked these soldiers.

In this painting by Edgar S. Paxon, Custer and his troopers, hopelessly surrounded by Sioux and Cheyenne warriors, fight to the death on Battle Ridge.

Then the Sioux and Cheyenne suddenly disappeared, and silence came at last.

The Indians retreated when they discovered the approach of Colonel Gibbon's army column. On June 27, Gibbon's men advanced into the valley and came upon the gruesome battlefield. "The stench from the dead bodies and dead horses was something terrible," exclaimed one stunned officer.[24] The stripped and mutilated bodies of Custer and his men lay where they had fallen. Many hands and feet had been cut off, and legs and bodies were stabbed and slashed. The dead soldiers could hardly be recognized. One sergeant was identified only because he still wore one sock with his name stitched on it. Lieutenant Calhoun's body was identified only by the fillings in his teeth. Tom Custer, his scalp gone, his skull crushed, was identified by a tattoo on his arm.

George Armstrong Custer's stripped body was found propped in a sitting position between two dead troopers behind a tangle of dead horses. He had been shot in the left temple and in the left side. All of Custer's 225 men had died with him. Five entire companies had been wiped out. "It was the most horrible sight my eyes rested on," said Lieutenant Francis Gibson.[25] In addition, Reno and Benteen had had fifty-three killed and sixty wounded. Perhaps one hundred Indians had died in the battle, including several women and children. Battlefield burial parties grimly dug graves.

Comanche

One survivor of the slaughter was Comanche, Captain Miles Keogh's horse. With at least seven wounds, Comanche had been left behind by the Indians. He recovered, and for the rest of his days appeared, saddled but unridden, with the 7th Cavalry Regiment on parade. He lived for fifteen more years and now stands stuffed under glass at the University of Kansas.[26]

Custer's Legacy

The Sioux and Cheyenne won a stunning victory at the Little Bighorn, their greatest victory in all the history of conflict between whites and the Great Plains Indians. Even today the Sioux call it *Pehin Hanska Ktepi*, the day "they killed Long Hair."[27] But to the United States, in the midst of the happy 1876 centennial celebration of American independence, the deaths of Custer and his men were shocking. In Washington, President Grant declared, "I regard Custer's massacre as a sacrifice of troops, brought on by Custer himself, that was wholly unnecessary—wholly unnecessary."[28] The Republican Chicago *Tribune* claimed that Custer had caused the disaster because he "preferred to make a reckless dash . . . in the hope of making a personal victory . . . rather than wait . . . and share the glory with others."[29] Libbie Custer was stunned by the news of her husband's death. Later, she confessed

that losing him was like the closing of "the windows of life that let in the sunshine."[30]

Many Americans blamed Major Reno for the defeat at the Little Bighorn. Publicly slandered, Reno demanded an inquiry into his conduct at the battle. A military trial finally cleared him of wrongdoing.

Although the Indians won a great battle in 1876, they eventually lost the war. Vengeful United States troops poured across the Northern Plains. Within a year, most of the Sioux and Cheyenne had surrendered. Sitting Bull and a small following took

After the battle, stones were erected to mark the sites where each of Custer's men fell. Most died either on Custer Hill or Calhoun Hill, both on Battle Ridge. In the distance, the Little Bighorn River flows among the trees.

refuge in Canada, but they, too, gave up in 1881. All were forced onto reservations.

Soldiers dug up Custer's body and shipped it east in July 1877. With bugles and speeches, he was buried with full military honors at West Point on October 10, 1877. Libbie Custer lived in New York City until her death on April 4, 1933, at the age of ninety. She was buried beside her husband. During her long life she wrote three books—*Boots and Saddles* (1885), *Tenting on the Plains* (1887), and *Following the Guidon* (1890)—all praising her husband's career.

Custer had yearned for fame and battlefield glory. But proud, vain, always reckless of danger, he had blindly led his men to final disaster. Controversy will forever swirl around the fight at the Little Bighorn, a battle better known as Custer's Last Stand. Fate had brought George Armstrong Custer to a place where he could die a spectacular soldier's death.

CHRONOLOGY

1839— Born in New Rumley, Ohio, on December 5, the son of Emanuel and Maria Custer.

1845— Begins attending school.

1852— Travels to Monroe, Michigan, to live with his half sister Ann Reed for three years.

1855— Attends the McNeely Normal School in Ohio.

1856— Becomes a schoolteacher in Cadiz, Ohio.

1857— Enters the United States Military Academy at West Point, New York.

1861— The American Civil War begins in April, after the Union surrender of Fort Sumter; Custer graduates from West Point in June at the bottom of his class; Is commissioned a second lieutenant and assigned to the 2nd United States Cavalry Regiment; Is present at the Battle of Bull Run on July 21.

1862— Is assigned to the staff of General W. F. Smith during the Peninsular Campaign in Virginia in April; Joins the staff of commanding General George McClellan in May as a brevet captain.

1863— Joins the staff of Brigadier General Alfred Pleasonton, commander of the 1st Cavalry Division, in May; Fights in cavalry battles at Brandy Station and at Aldie in June; Is promoted to the brevet rank of brigadier general on June 28, and is given command of the Michigan Brigade; Leads the brigade at the Battle of Gettysburg in Pennsylvania, July 2–3; Fights at Falling Waters, Maryland, July 14; Fights at Brandy Station and Buckland Mills, Virginia, in October.

1864— Marries Elizabeth Bacon in Monroe, Michigan, on February 9; Makes a successful raid toward Charlottesville, Virginia, in March; Michigan Brigade becomes part of Major General Philip Sheridan's Cavalry Corps in March; Fights at Yellow Tavern in May and at Trevilian Station in June; As part of Sheridan's Army of the Shenandoah, fights at Opequon Creek in September; Is given command of the 3rd Cavalry Division; Fights at Tom's Brook and Cedar Creek in October; Is promoted to the brevet rank of major general.

1865— Fights at Waynesboro and at Five Forks in March and at Sayler's Creek in April; Assists in the pursuit of Robert E. Lee's Confederate Army to Appomattox; Robert E. Lee surrenders his army to Ulysses S. Grant, April 9; Takes part in the Grand Review, a victory parade in Washington, D.C., in May.

1866— Is assigned to the 7th Cavalry Regiment as a lieutenant colonel; Is stationed at Fort Riley, Kansas.

1867— Takes part in the Hancock expedition against Indians on the Southern Plains; Is court-martialed for being absent without leave from his command.

1868— Is restored to duty; Attacks Cheyenne Indians at the Battle of Washita in November.

1869— Persuades Arapaho and Cheyenne to surrender without fighting in January and March.

1871— While on duty in Elizabethtown, Kentucky, writes articles for *Galaxy* magazine.

1873— Takes part in the Yellowstone expedition, accompanying a railroad surveying party on the Northern Plains; Skirmishes with Sioux Indians in July and August; Takes command of Fort Abraham Lincoln in the Dakota Territory.

1874— Leads an expedition to explore the Black Hills region of the Dakotas in July and August.

1876— In May, joins an expedition to conquer hostile Sioux and Cheyenne in the Yellowstone region; Sets out with the 7th Cavalry on June 22, headed toward the Little Bighorn River; Is killed fighting the Sioux and Cheyenne at the Battle of the Little Bighorn on June 25, along with all of the 225 troopers who rode with him.

1877— Is buried at West Point.

CHAPTER NOTES

Chapter 1. The Little Bighorn

1. Gregory J. W. Urwin, *Custer Victorious* (Lincoln: University of Nebraska Press, 1983), p. 36.

2. Frederic Franklyn Van de Water, *Glory-Hunter: A Life of General Custer* (New York: Bobbs Merrill Co., 1934), p. 334.

3. James Welch, *Killing Custer* (New York: W. W. Norton & Company, 1994), p. 128.

4. Jeffrey D. Wert, *Custer* (New York: Simon & Schuster, 1996), p. 344.

5. Ibid.

6. Ibid., p. 349.

7. Van de Water, p. 346.

8. Wert, p. 351.

9. Urwin, p. 59.

Chapter 2. A Cadet at West Point

1. Jeffrey D. Wert, *Custer* (New York: Simon & Schuster, 1996), p. 18.

2. Ibid., p. 21.

3. Elizabeth Bacon Custer, *The Civil War Memories of Elizabeth Bacon Custer* (Austin: University of Texas Press, 1994), pp. 11–12.

4. George Armstrong Custer, *Custer in the Civil War, His Unfinished Memoirs*, ed. John M. Carroll (San Rafael, Calif.: Presidio Press, 1977), p. 78.

5. Wert, p. 27.

6. Ibid., p. 29.

7. Gregory J. W. Urwin, "From West Point to the Battlefield," *The Custer Reader*, ed. Paul Andrew Hutton (Lincoln: University of Nebraska Press, 1992), p. 9.

8. Wert, p. 30.

9. Ibid., p. 32.

10. Urwin, p. 9.

11. Wert, p. 36.

12. George Armstrong Custer, p. 82.

13. Alan Aimone and Barbara Aimone, "Much to Sadden—and Little to Cheer," *Blue & Gray*, December 1991, p. 24.

14. Wert, p. 38.

15. George Armstrong Custer, p. 88.

Chapter 3. Young Cavalry Officer

1. George Armstrong Custer, *Custer in the Civil War, His Unfinished Memoirs*, ed. John M. Carroll (San Rafael, Calif.: Presidio Press, 1977), p. 93.

2. Ibid., p. 102.

3. Ibid., pp. 100–101.

4. Gregory J. W. Urwin, *Custer Victorious* (Lincoln: University of Nebraska Press, 1983), p. 46.

5. George Armstrong Custer, p. 110.

6. Ibid., p. 143.

7. Ibid., pp. 146–148.

8. Jeffrey D. Wert, *Custer* (New York: Simon & Schuster, 1996), p. 52.

9. George Armstrong Custer, p. 1.

10. Elizabeth Bacon Custer, *The Civil War Memories of Elizabeth Bacon Custer* (Austin: University of Texas Press, 1994), p. 76.

11. Wert, p. 69.

12. Ibid., p. 75.

13. Urwin, p. 53.

14. Frederic Franklyn Van de Water, *Glory-Hunter: A Life of General Custer* (New York: Bobbs Merrill Co., 1934), p. 51.

15. Gregory J. W. Urwin, "From West Point to the Battlefield," *The Custer Reader*, ed. Paul Andrew Hutton (Lincoln: University of Nebraska Press, 1992), p. 15.

Chapter 4. Custer Earns His Star

1. J. H. Kidd, *Riding with Custer* (Lincoln: University of Nebraska Press, 1997), p. 129.

2. Jeffrey D. Wert, *Custer* (New York: Simon & Schuster, 1996), p. 85.

3. Gregory J. W. Urwin, *Custer Victorious* (Lincoln: University of Nebraska Press, 1983), p. 70.

4. Gregory J. W. Urwin, "From West Point to the Battlefield," *The Custer Reader*, ed. Paul Andrew Hutton (Lincoln: University of Nebraska Press, 1992), p. 16.

5. Ibid., p. 17.

6. Ibid.

7. Wert, p. 105.

8. Urwin, *Custer Victorious*, p. 95.

9. Lawrence A. Frost, *General Custer's Libbie* (Seattle: Superior Publishing Co., 1976), p. 80.

10. Urwin, *Custer Victorious*, p. 102.

11. Ibid., pp. 102–103.

12. Marguerite Merington, ed., *The Custer Story: The Life and Intimate Letters of General George A. Custer and His Wife Elizabeth* (New York: Devin-Adair Co., 1950), p. 68.

13. Elizabeth Bacon Custer, *The Civil War Memories of Elizabeth Bacon Custer* (Austin: University of Texas Press, 1994), p. 54.

14. Wert, p. 150.

Chapter 5. Philip Sheridan Takes Command

1. Jeffrey D. Wert, *Custer* (New York: Simon & Schuster, 1996), p. 153.

2. Ibid., p. 154.

3. Gregory J. W. Urwin, *Custer Victorious* (Lincoln: University of Nebraska Press, 1983), p. 164.

4. Ibid., p. 169.

5. Wert, p. 171.

6. Urwin, *Custer Victorious*, p. 186.

7. George Armstrong Custer, *Custer in the Civil War, His Unfinished Memoirs*, ed. John M. Carroll (San Rafael, Calif.: Presidio Press, 1977), p. 38.

8. Frederic Franklyn Van de Water, *Glory-Hunter: A Life of General Custer* (New York: Bobbs Merrill Co., 1934), p. 84.

9. Urwin, *Custer Victorious*, p. 199.

10. Gregory J. W. Urwin, "From West Point to the Battlefield," *The Custer Reader*, ed. Paul Andrew Hutton (Lincoln: University of Nebraska Press, 1992), p. 22.

11. Urwin, *Custer Victorious*, p. 202.

12. Ibid., p. 210.

13. John B. Gordon, *Reminiscences of the Civil War* (New York: Charles Scribner's Sons, 1903), p. 348.

14. Custer, p. 46.

15. Urwin, *Custer Victorious*, p. 215.

16. Ibid., p. 30.

Chapter 6. Pursuit to Appomattox

1. Jeffrey D. Wert, *Custer* (New York: Simon & Schuster, 1996), p. 213.

2. Marguerite Merington, ed., *The Custer Story: The Life and Intimate Letters of General George A. Custer and His Wife Elizabeth* (New York: Devin-Adair Co., 1950), pp. 140–141.

3. Gregory J. W. Urwin, "From West Point to the Battlefield," *The Custer Reader*, ed. Paul Andrew Hutton (Lincoln: University of Nebraska Press, 1992), p. 23.

4. Urwin, *Custer Victorious*, p. 254.

5. James Longstreet, *From Manassas to Appomattox* (New York: Da Capo Press, 1992), p. 627.

6. Elizabeth Bacon Custer, *The Civil War Memories of Elizabeth Bacon Custer* (Austin: University of Texas Press, 1994), p. 151.

7. Ibid., p. 143.

8. Ibid., p. 162.

Chapter 7. Custer of the 7th Cavalry

1. Jeffrey D. Wert, *Custer* (New York: Simon & Schuster, 1996), p. 245.

2. Ibid., p. 250.

3. Frederic Franklyn Van de Water, *Glory-Hunter: A Life of General Custer* (New York: Bobbs Merrill Co., 1934), p. 159.

4. George Armstrong Custer, *My Life on the Plains* (Lincoln: University of Nebraska Press, 1952), p. 95.

5. Wert, p. 255.

6. Brian W. Dippie, "Custer: The Indian Fighter," *The Custer Reader*, ed. Paul Andrew Hutton (Lincoln: University of Nebraska Press, 1992), p. 105.

7. Custer, p. 70.

8. Ibid., pp. 197–198.

9. Minnie Dubbs Millbrook, "The West Breaks in General Custer," *The Custer Reader*, ed. Paul Andrew Hutton (Lincoln: University of Nebraska Press, 1992), p. 145.

10. Ibid.

Chapter 8. Return to the Southern Plains

1. George Armstrong Custer, *My Life on the Plains* (Lincoln: University of Nebraska Press, 1952), p. 216.

2. Jeffrey D. Wert, *Custer* (New York: Simon & Schuster, 1996), p. 267.

3. Brian W. Dippie, "Custer: The Indian Fighter," *The Custer Reader*, ed. Paul Andrew Hutton (Lincoln: University of Nebraska Press, 1992), p. 106.

4. Marguerite Merington, ed., *The Custer Story: The Life and Intimate Letters of General George A. Custer and His Wife Elizabeth* (New York: Devin-Adair Co., 1950), p. 217.

5. Frederic Franklyn Van de Water, *Glory-Hunter: A Life of General Custer* (New York: Bobbs Merrill Co., 1934), p. 188.

6. Custer, p. 289.

7. Wert, p. 274.

8. Custer, p. 335.

9. Ibid.

10. Ibid., p. 338.

11. James Welch, *Killing Custer* (New York: W. W. Norton & Company, 1994), p. 57.

12. Edward S. Godfrey, "Some Reminiscences, Including the Washita Battle, November 27, 1868," *The Custer Reader*, ed. Paul Andrew Hutton (Lincoln: University of Nebraska Press, 1992), p. 171.

13. Custer, p. 347.

14. Godfrey, p. 173.

15. Kate Bighead, "She Watched Custer's Last Battle," as told to Thomas B. Marquis, *The Custer Reader*, ed. Paul Andrew Hutton (Lincoln: University of Nebraska Press, 1992), p. 363.

16. Wert, p. 280.

17. Custer, p. 425.

18. Wert, p. 285.

Chapter 9. On the Northern Plains

1. Elizabeth B. Custer, *Boots and Saddles* (Norman: University of Oklahoma Press, 1961), p. 4.

2. Jeffrey D. Wert, *Custer* (New York: Simon & Schuster, 1996), p. 296.

3. Charles W. Larned, "Letters of a Young Cavalry Officer," ed. George Frederick Howe, *The Custer Reader*, ed. Paul Andrew Hutton (Lincoln: University of Nebraska Press, 1992), p. 184.

4. Wert, p. 299.

5. Ibid., p. 300.

6. Ibid., p. 301.

7. Ibid., p. 303.

8. Mary Elizabeth Sergent, "Classmates Divided," *American Heritage*, February 1958, p. 35.

9. G. A. Custer, "Battling with the Sioux on the Yellowstone," *The Custer Reader*, ed. Paul Andrew Hutton (Lincoln: University of Nebraska Press, 1992), p. 209.

10. Wert, p. 308.

11. Ibid., p. 313.

12. Brian W. Dippie, "Custer: The Indian Fighter," *The Custer Reader*, ed. Paul Andrew Hutton (Lincoln: University of Nebraska Press, 1992), p. 110.

13. Frederic Franklyn Van de Water, *Glory-Hunter: A Life of General Custer* (New York: Bobbs Merrill Co., 1934), p. 261.

Chapter 10. Custer's Last Stand

1. Frederic Franklyn Van de Water, *Glory-Hunter: A Life of General Custer* (New York: Bobbs Merrill Co., 1934), p. 291.

2. Ibid., p. 300.

3. Elizabeth B. Custer, *Boots and Saddles* (Norman: University of Oklahoma Press, 1961), p. 275.

4. James Welch, *Killing Custer* (New York: W. W. Norton & Company, 1994), p. 51.

5. Jeffrey D. Wert, *Custer* (New York: Simon & Schuster, 1996), p. 335.

6. Van de Water, p. 319.

7. Wert, pp. 339–340.

8. Welch, p. 152.

9. Van de Water, p. 339.

10. Wert, p. 345.

11. Kate Bighead, "She Watched Custer's Last Battle," (as told to Thomas B. Marquis), *The Custer Reader*, ed. Paul Andrew Hutton (Lincoln: University of Nebraska Press, 1992), p. 366.

12. Edward S. Godfrey, "Custer's Last Battle," *The Custer Reader*, ed. Paul Andrew Hutton (Lincoln: University of Nebraska Press, 1992), p. 287.

13. David Humphreys Miller, "Echoes of the Little Bighorn," *American Heritage*, June 1991, p. 31.

14. Welch, p. 161.

15. Stanley Vestal, "The Man Who Killed Custer," *American Heritage*, February 1957, p. 8.

16. Wert, p. 351.

17. Miller, p. 38.

18. John Stands In Timber, "Last Ghastly Moments at the Little Big Horn," *American Heritage*, April 1966, p. 21.

19. Wert, p. 353.

20. Vestal, p. 9.

21. Miller, p. 36.

22. Bighead, p. 372.

23. Miller, p. 34.

24. Wert, p. 354.

25. Ibid.

26. Welch, p. 174.

27. Wert, p. 353.

28. Paul Andrew Hutton, *The Custer Reader* (Lincoln: University of Nebraska Press, 1992), p. 388.

29. Ibid., p. 398.

30. Elizabeth Bacon Custer, *The Civil War Memories of Elizabeth Bacon Custer* (Austin: University of Texas Press, 1994), p. xi.

GLOSSARY

adjutant—A military staff officer who assists the commanding officer in issuing orders.

annals—A record of events.

battalion—A military unit made up of a headquarters and two or more companies.

bluff—A cliff or hill with a broad, steep face.

brigade—A military unit consisting of two or more regiments or battalions.

buzzard—A large, meat-eating bird.

caisson—A two-wheeled ammunition wagon for artillery.

captivate—To charm or enchant.

cavalry—A military force of soldiers on horseback.

centennial—A hundredth anniversary.

chaos—A state of complete confusion or disorder.

charger—A horse suitable to be ridden into battle.

color-bearer—A person who carries the flag of a military unit.

corps—A military unit consisting of two or more divisions.

coulee—A deep ravine or gulch.

curdle—(to make one's blood curdle) To thicken or freeze with terror.

delegate—A person chosen to represent others.

demerit—A mark against a person for bad conduct.

depot—A railroad station.

division—A military unit consisting of two or more brigades.

engineer—A person educated in the design, construction, and operation of engines, machines, railroads, bridges, and so on.

ethics—Rules of conduct; morals.

fatigue—Weariness.

flank—The side of anything.

foundry—A factory where metal is cast into forms.

fray—A noisy quarrel, fight, skirmish, or battle.

furlough—A vacation granted to a military person.

generator—A machine that converts one form of energy into another.

geology—The study of the earth's rock formations.

hanker—To long for.

headwaters—The sources of a river.

hydrogen—The lightest of the known elements; a colorless, odorless, flammable gas.

invincible—Incapable of being conquered or defeated.

legacy—A gift or history left behind.

orderly—A military servant who carries messages and performs other personal duties for an officer.

peninsula—Land bordered on three sides by water.

ration—A fixed allowance of food.

rebuke—Stern disapproval.

regiment—A military unit made up of a number of battalions.

resolute—Firmly determined.

secede—To withdraw from an alliance or union.

skirmish—A brisk fight between small groups of enemies.

slander—To hurt by making false statements.

taxidermist—One who preserves the skins of animals by stuffing them in lifelike form.

teamster—The driver of a team of horses.

wolverine—A black, long-haired, meat-eating mammal; the mascot of the state of Michigan.

FURTHER READING

Books

Custer, George Armstrong. *My Life on the Plains.* Lincoln: University of Nebraska Press, 1952.

Ferrell, Nancy Warren. *The Battle of the Little Bighorn in American History.* Springfield, N.J.: Enslow Publishers, Inc., 1996.

Guttmacher, Peter. *Crazy Horse, Sioux War Chief.* New York: Chelsea House, 1994.

Kent, Zachary. *The Civil War: "A House Divided."* Hillside, N.J.: Enslow Publishers, Inc., 1994.

Lewis, Thomas A. *The Shenandoah in Flames: The Valley Campaign of 1864.* Alexandria, Va.: Time-Life Books, Inc., 1987.

Schleichert, Elizabeth. *Sitting Bull.* Springfield, N.J.: Enslow Publishers, Inc., 1997.

Stein, R. Conrad. *The Story of the Little Bighorn.* Chicago: Children's Press, 1983.

Wert, Jeffrey D. *Custer.* New York: Simon & Schuster, 1996.

Internet Addresses

Monroe County Library System. *George Armstrong Custer.* February 13, 1998. <http://monroe.lib.mi.us/custer.htm> (May 27, 1999).

North Dakota State Parks. *Fort Abraham Lincoln State Park.* November 25, 1998. <http://www.state.nd.us.ndparks/Parks/Lincoln/Lincoln.htm> (May 27, 1999).

U.S. Army Combined Arms Center, Fort Leavenworth, Kansas. "The Court Martial of George Armstrong Custer." *Fort Leavenworth History.* August 1997. <http://leav-www.army.mil.history/custer.htm> (May 27, 1999).

INDEX